Golgotha

Golgotha

ANDREW C. SKINNER

DESERET
BOOK

SALT LAKE CITY, UTAH

Library of Congress Cataloging-in-Publication Data

Skinner, Andrew C., 1951–
   Golgotha / Andrew C. Skinner.
       p.   cm.
   Includes bibliographical references and index.
   ISBN 1-57008-962-0 (alk. paper)
   1. Jesus Christ—Mormon interpretations.   2. Jesus Christ—Biography—Passion Week.   3. Church of Jesus Christ of Latter-day Saints—Doctrines.   I. Title.
   BX8643.J4 S55 2003
   232.96—dc22   2003019731

Printed in the United States of America   72076
Publishers Printing, Salt Lake City, UT

10   9   8   7   6   5   4   3   2

For family and friends,
who continue to teach me about God's love

Contents

Introduction

Golgotha is a necessary sequel to *Gethsemane*, for what began in the Garden of Gethsemane was completed on the cross of Golgotha and ultimately in the Garden Tomb. In Gethsemane Jesus of Nazareth absorbed to himself all of the sins, sorrows, sufferings, and heartaches of the whole human family—those living on this earth and on countless others like it. In Gethsemane he confronted horrors the likes of which most of us may glimpse but not really comprehend. In Gethsemane Jesus became us, so to speak, each one of us, so that we can become like him (2 Corinthians 5:21). In Gethsemane Jesus consumed the bitter cup so that we will not have to. But Gethsemane was not the end of the bitter cup. At Golgotha the bitter cup was refilled and drunk again. In the economy of the universe, Golgotha had to follow Gethsemane. Without Golgotha Gethsemane would have been incomplete. As Elder Bruce R. McConkie noted, "In some way, incomprehensible to us, Gethsemane, the cross, and the empty tomb join into one grand and eternal drama, in the course of which Jesus abolishes death, and out of which comes immortality for all and eternal life for the righteous" (*Mortal Messiah*, 4:224).

The essence of Golgotha for the Savior was abandonment in the face of treachery and malicious treatment. The lesson of Golgotha for us is meekness and character—the pure, unadulterated, unparalleled personality and makeup of our Lord. Golgotha is as profound a story of unsurpassed concern for others in the face of violence and vileness as will ever be found. Even in the throes of death, when he was experiencing the greatest suffering and most undeserved treatment ever known, the Savior of the universe was thinking of others—his family, his associates, all of us, and his literal Father (our Father in Heaven). In my lifetime I have both seen and heard of the kind of character possessed by the Savior, who took what was meted out solely for the sake of others and the kingdom of God. Those modern examples have helped me to understand more clearly what was truly accomplished on a far greater scale at Golgotha.

Years ago, as a full-time missionary for The Church of Jesus Christ of Latter-day Saints, I was told by a trustworthy source about a man who had been called to serve a mission in the Southern States many decades before. He arrived in the mission field only to find out from the president that his companion's arrival would be delayed. Therefore, he was asked to go alone to a certain town and do what he could until a companion could join him. (Things were a little less formal in those days.) He accepted the assignment, went to the town (which had not seen missionaries for a long time), and began to look for odd jobs or community service projects. He hoped that by doing so he could create some goodwill in the community and thereby establish a foundation of relationships upon which he and his future companion could build.

A few days passed, and still no companion arrived. Word began to spread that the Mormons were in town—and they were not welcome. When this elder returned to his lodgings at night, usually without having found any townsfolk interested even in free labor, he began to be accosted in the back streets and alleyways by the local bullies. He defended himself as best he could—sometimes even admirably (he had been a boxer before he entered the mission field)—but he could not fend off three or four opponents at a time. He became discouraged and felt completely abandoned. To be beaten up every night was depressing and painful. But to suffer unjust punishment for something good he was trying to accomplish, something that had been asked of him by Church leaders, was truly demoralizing and a challenge to his faith.

Nevertheless, he hung on and prayed every day that the Lord would hurry and send him a companion. Years later he said that he had told the Lord he didn't care one bit if the companion knew anything about the gospel, "just let him be a fighter!"

The message of this missionary's deeds had a powerful and profound effect on me, who many decades later was trying to muster enough gumption and maturity to go forth and be a powerful servant like the one in the story. I did not immediately make any connection with the Savior or Golgotha. The missionary in the story was purely a hero to me then. But in the years that have followed, I have come to see that this missionary was more like the Savior than I fathomed at the time. I had not yet read Doctrine and Covenants 138, Joseph F. Smith's 1918 vision of the redemption of the dead, because it was not at that time part of our official canon (it was adopted as part of the standard works in 1976). Since then, however, I have come to see the connection between the Savior's enduring sacrifice and

the sacrifice of the missionary in the story—and, in fact, the
connection between the Savior on the cross at Golgotha and
the sacrifices of all the righteous in any age who offer their best
in the face of malicious treatment, feelings of being abandoned
by God, depression, demoralizing challenges, destitution, hardship, or other tribulations. The missionary in the story was an
illustration of, indeed a similitude of, Jesus' experience at
Golgotha. As President Joseph F. Smith saw in vision:

> There were gathered together in one place an innumer-
> able company of the spirits of the just, who had been
> faithful in the testimony of Jesus while they lived in
> mortality;
>   And who had offered sacrifice in the similitude of the
> great sacrifice of the Son of God, and had suffered tribu-
> lation in their Redeemer's name. (D&C 138:12–13)

Ultimately, the circumstances of the missionary in the story
did come to some resolution. One day he received a telegram
from the mission president indicating that he was to meet a
companion at the train station at such and such a time. He
went to the station with some hope, but that feeling changed
back to hopelessness as passenger after passenger filed off the
train without any sign of a missionary companion. As the last
of the passengers departed, he was turning away in despair when
out of the corner of his eye, he caught a glimpse of something
shiny. He turned to see what it was. Staring him in the face was
the biggest belt buckle he had ever seen in his life. Filling the
doorframe of the railroad car was the figure of a six-foot-six-
inch-tall cowboy from Wyoming—his new companion.
Immediately things began to look up (in more ways than one)!

I do not recall hearing that the set of missionaries had any success in that place, at least as success is measured by baptisms. I do remember hearing that the missionaries "began to clean up the town." As it turned out, the missionary from Wyoming had grown up on a ranch, roping and wrestling cattle. A few town bullies did not intimidate him. I remember thinking at the time that God always hears and answers the prayers of his servants. I still have a conviction that such a doctrine is true, but I have also come to know that storybook endings do not always occur in mortality. Rather, God honors and rewards the sacrifices of those who love him, whether in this life or in the next. He is able to do so precisely because of the infinite sacrifice of his Beloved Son, who, after experiencing Gethsemane, did not shrink from Golgotha but saw it through to its end and thus was willing to forgo a happy ending in mortality to ensure a happy ending in eternity.

Ultimately, all of our hopes, dreams, and righteous desires come down to the meekness and character of Christ. I hope that the story of Golgotha as told in the following pages will increase our appreciation for the meekness and character of the sinless Son of God. The story of Golgotha leaves us with the lasting impression that all things truly testify of Christ, for all of Israelite history, prophecy, ritual, symbolism, and religious institutions pointed to the Savior and were fulfilled in him.

And while he yet spake, lo, Judas, one of the twelve, came, and with him a great multitude with swords and staves, from the chief priests and elders of the people.

Now he that betrayed him gave them a sign, saying, Whomsoever I shall kiss, that same is he: hold him fast.

And forthwith he came to Jesus, and said, Hail, master; and kissed him.

And Jesus said unto him, Friend, wherefore art thou come? Then came they, and laid hands on Jesus, and took him.

And, behold, one of them which were with Jesus stretched out his hand, and drew his sword, and struck a servant of the high priest's, and smote off his ear.

MATTHEW 26:47–51

CHAPTER 1

Betrayal and Arrest

We do not know how long Jesus endured the agony of Gethsemane, but surely its toll is to be measured in intensity rather than simply length. The noted English theologian and biographer of Christ, Frederic Farrar, called Gethsemane "a grief beyond utterance, a struggle beyond endurance, a horror of great darkness. . . . how dreadful was that paroxysm of prayer and suffering through which He passed" (*Life of Christ*, 553).

From a purely human perspective, it must have looked as though the bloodied and tear-stained Son of God suffered nothing more than the tragedy and disgrace of emotional break-down. After all, the Messiah was supposed to be a conqueror, not a sufferer, and the apostles knew it—else why would they "be sore amazed, and . . . be very heavy, and . . . complain in their hearts, wondering if this be the Messiah" (JST Mark 14:36).

But the Savior was not out to impress either onlookers or associates. He was focused singly on doing his Father's will, even when it meant that divine wrath had to be poured out on the

7

Son because he was absorbing for us the eternal punishments deserved for every law mankind has ever broken. "Jesus always deserved and always had the Father's full approval. But when He took our sins upon Him, of divine necessity required by justice He experienced instead 'the fierceness of the wrath of Almighty God' (D&C 76:107; 88:106)" (Maxwell, *Lord, Increase Our Faith*, 13). In Gethsemane Jesus suffered the wrath of God—the wrath of divine justice—so that we do not have to. He suffered the wrath and ravages of spiritual death and hell so that you and I can escape it. As President Joseph Fielding Smith said:

> Jesus did come into the world to ransom it. Through his atonement we were bought from death and hell. Death and hell were paid—paid in full—and Christ was the only one who could pay that debt. . . .
>
> . . . He carried, in some way that I cannot understand and you cannot understand, the burden of the combined weight of the sins of the world. It is hard enough for me to carry my own transgressions, and it is hard enough for you to carry yours. . . . I have seen [people] cry out in anguish because of their transgressions—just one individual's sins. Can you comprehend the suffering of Jesus Christ when he carried, not merely by physical manifestation but in some spiritual and mental condition or manner, the combined weight of sin? . . .
>
> . . . This extreme suffering—which was beyond the power of mortal man either to accomplish or endure—was undertaken because of the great love which the Father and the Son had for mankind. (*Doctrines of Salvation*, 1:125, 129–30, 131)

Sin brings divine wrath because God cannot tolerate sin or look upon it with the least degree of allowance (D&C 1:31), nor can sin be tolerated in a universe framed by the perfect, pure, and fair law of justice. God's physical makeup, his holiness and purity, make it impossible for him to tolerate or withstand any kind of sinful environment. Christ's atonement removes from us the intolerable taint or stain of sin.

From an eternal perspective, we know that when Jesus had finished praying the same prayer three times in Gethsemane, he had gained a victory of monumental, unequaled proportions. He had fulfilled perfectly his Father's will up to that point, knowing even then that he had yet to face the agony of the cross and drain again the dregs of the bitter cup refilled.

THE KISS OF BETRAYAL

The Gospel writers tell us that as Jesus addressed his sleeping apostles for the final time in the Garden of Gethsemane after he had finished praying, he was met by a multitude of chief priests and elders—the police force of the Jerusalem Temple—brandishing weapons and led by none other than Judas Iscariot, one of the Twelve Apostles, who was to identify Jesus by the prearranged signal of a kiss (Matthew 26:48). So began a series of exhausting events after an already long night, events that culminated in the Crucifixion, events that provide us with a profound lesson in loyalty.

John's unique account of events that occurred after Jesus concluded his time in Gethsemane reminds us that Judas knew where to find Jesus during those wee hours of the morning because "Jesus ofttimes resorted thither with his disciples" (John 18:2). In other words, Jesus had gone often to Gethsemane on several occasions *before* his atoning act, and Judas knew it. Even more significant, John alone describes the remarkable scene that indicates Judas's kiss was not the sole mark of identification but that Jesus proactively initiated an exchange between himself and his stalkers:

> Jesus therefore, knowing all things that should come upon him, went forth, and said unto them, Whom seek ye?
>
> They answered him, Jesus of Nazareth. Jesus saith unto them, *I am* he. And Judas also, which betrayed him, stood with them.
>
> As soon then as he had said unto them, *I am* he, they went backward, and fell to the ground.
>
> Then asked he them again, Whom seek ye? And they said, Jesus of Nazareth.
>
> Jesus answered, I have told you that *I am* he: if therefore ye seek me, let these go their way:
>
> That the saying might be fulfilled, which he spake, Of them which thou gavest me have I lost none.
>
> Then Simon Peter having a sword drew it, and smote the high priest's servant, and cut off his right ear. The servant's name was Malchus. (John 18:4–10; emphasis added)

The tone of this episode seems to indicate that in Gethsemane's dark shadows Jesus was not immediately recognized, hence the response of the arresting mob to Jesus' question about whom they were seeking. They do not say, "It is you we are seeking." They say, "Jesus of Nazareth." In the darkness Jesus did not immediately look appreciably different from the apostles surrounding him. But Jesus was no shy or retiring leader. Neither did he fear his captors. He boldly identified himself to the mob by using language that equated him with God—"I Am." That is the very name of Deity as revealed to Moses (Exodus 3:13–14). The translators of the King James Version of the Bible added the word *he* after each use of the phrase "I Am" in this passage, believing it rounded out the translation. Without that added word, however, we can understand more readily why the chief priests and elders responded as they did, for when they heard Jesus utter those words, they fell backward to the ground—as might anyone who has had the wind knocked out of him because God himself has just responded to his inquiry. To say that Jesus' words were shocking to the chief priests and elders is an understatement of greatest proportion. We suppose that it was not only *what* Jesus said but *how* he said it. That is, the force of Jesus' response, indeed his very presence and power of personality, had a stunning effect on the armed mob: Jesus spoke with heavenly power.

Elder Parley P. Pratt witnessed a similar scene when he was incarcerated in Richmond, Missouri, with Joseph Smith. Like Jesus, the Prophet had been betrayed into the hands of enemies by a trusted associate. One evening in the jail, Elder Pratt saw the Prophet Joseph speak with the same kind of power that had caused Jesus' captors to fall backwards in stunned silence, overcome by the force of Jesus' words. Elder Pratt described his experience:

> In one of those tedious nights we had lain as if in sleep till the hour of midnight had passed, and our ears and hearts had been pained, while we had listened for hours to the obscene jests, the horrid oaths, the dreadful blasphemies and filthy language of our guards . . . as they recounted to each other their deeds of rapine,

murder, robbery, etc., which they had committed among the "*Mormons*" while at Far West and vicinity. They even boasted of defiling by force wives, daughters, and virgins, and of shooting or dashing out the brains of men, women and children.

I had listened till I became so disgusted, shocked, horrified, and so filled with the spirit of indignant justice, that I could scarcely refrain from rising upon my feet and rebuking the guards; but had said nothing to Joseph, or anyone else, although I lay next to him and knew he was awake. On a sudden he arose to his feet, and spoke in a voice of thunder, or as the roaring lion, uttering, as near as I can recollect, the following words:

'*SILENCE, ye fiends of the infernal pit. In the name of Jesus Christ I rebuke you, and command you to be still. I will not live another minute and bear such language. Cease such talk, or you or I die THIS INSTANT!*'

He ceased to speak. He stood erect in terrible majesty. Chained, and without a weapon; calm, unruffled and dignified as an angel, he looked upon the quailing guards . . . whose knees smote together, and who, shrinking into a corner, or crouching at his feet, begged his pardon, and remained quiet till a change of guards.

I have seen ministers of justice, clothed in magisterial robes, and criminals arraigned before them, while life was suspended on a breath, in the Courts of England; I have witnessed a Congress in solemn session to give laws to nations; I have tried to conceive of kings, of royal courts, of thrones and crowns; and of emperors assembled to decide the fate of kingdoms; but dignity and majesty have I seen but *once*, as it stood in chains, at midnight, in a dungeon in an obscure village of Missouri. (Pratt, *Autobiography*, 262–63)

Dignity and *majesty* are words that truly describe the Savior on the night of his arrest, even though he was in his extremity, suffering incomprehensibly, and surrounded by armed assailants, just as the Prophet Joseph Smith would be.

The Synoptic Gospels report that Judas did step forward and verify the identity of his Master by kissing him, but they make no mention of Jesus' identifying himself to the armed mob as the Gospel of John does. Nonetheless, Judas's kiss has become the hallmark event of the night of betrayal. That there is exact and pointed agreement among the Synoptics regarding Judas's position as a member of the Quorum of the Twelve Apostles perhaps reflects the shock and intensity with which that moment was felt by those disciples present. Surely the fact that Judas held the keys of the apostleship, along with the other special witnesses, added to the Savior's grief as Judas singled him out. After all, do we not learn that in all dispensations of time loyalty to one's brethren always was and always will be essential? (Proverbs 6:16, 19; John 17:11; D&C 38:27). There seem to be few things that the Lord abhors more than disloyalty. Conversely, there are few things as highly prized as loyalty and true friendship. The Prophet Joseph Smith said on one occasion:

> I don't care what a man's character is; if he's my friend—a true friend, I will be a friend to him, and preach the Gospel of salvation to him, and give him good counsel, helping him out of his difficulties.
>
> Friendship is one of the grand fundamental principles of 'Mormonism'; [it is designed] to revolutionize

and civilize the world, and cause wars and contentions to cease and men to become friends and brothers. . . .

It is a time-honored adage that love begets love. Let us pour forth love—show forth our kindness unto all mankind, and the Lord will reward us with everlasting increase; cast our bread upon the waters and we shall receive it after many days, increased to a hundredfold. (*Teachings of the Prophet Joseph Smith,* 316)

The great kiss of betrayal evokes an irony matched by few other episodes. By New Testament times, a kiss in public was a symbol both of distinction and of elevation. Among the ancient Israelites, a kiss often signified reconciliation between separated or estranged parties, as when Esau ran to Jacob after a long and wrenching conflict and "embraced him, and fell on his neck, and kissed him: and they wept" (Genesis 33:4). After years of separation, Joseph "kissed all his brethren, and wept upon them: and after that his brethren talked with him" (Genesis 45:15). When the Lord sent Aaron to meet Moses, he found him "in the mount of God, and kissed him" (Exodus 4:27).

Among the later Jews, a kiss was a token of respect with which pupils or disciples greeted their great rabbis or teachers. Among Christians, a kiss was a demonstration of fellowship and brotherhood. When he was visiting Simon the Pharisee's house, the Savior rebuked Simon, saying, "Thou gavest me no kiss" (Luke 7:45). The apostle Paul counseled early Church brethren to "greet all the brethren with an holy kiss" (1 Thessalonians 5:26). In our own day, one recalls that President Spencer W. Kimball was fond of greeting some of his associates and friends with a kiss on the cheek. I vividly remember a teenage friend telling me of walking along a street in downtown Salt Lake City with his father several years before. All of a sudden there was a flurry of activity as an energetic old man came running across the street, stopping traffic, walking up to his father, and greeting him with a kiss on the cheek. Much to my friend's surprise, he found himself staring at President Kimball. My friend's father had been called as a stake president several years earlier by then-Elder Kimball, and they had remained close friends. President Kimball's kiss was a tangible sign of his respect and affection.

The custom of greeting special friends with a kiss is still current in certain Middle Eastern countries. A few years ago, I was with a group of American students in Egypt, waiting for a guide who would take us to some archaeological sites. As it turned out, the guide assigned to us that day was a wonderful man who had become a friend through the years. Therefore, when he arrived, he immediately walked over to me and kissed me on both cheeks, much to the surprise of the students gathered in the parking lot of our Cairo hotel.

Proverbs 27:6 thus becomes even more poignant as we reflect on the episode involving Judas Iscariot in the Garden of Gethsemane that awful Thursday night: "Faithful are the wounds of a friend: but the kisses of an enemy are deceitful." How the kiss from Judas must have stung the Savior as he remembered the verse from Proverbs. And how Judas must have been taken aback by the Savior's rejoinders: "*Friend,* wherefore are thou come?" (Matthew 26:50; emphasis added) and "Betrayest thou the Son of Man with a kiss?" (Luke 22:48). Could a greater indictment of guilt have been leveled at Judas than with the single word *friend?* Or could there have been a greater expression of devastated disappointment uttered than the question, "You're betraying me with a *kiss?*"

The Greek word Matthew used to describe Judas's kiss, *kataphileo*, means "to kiss earnestly, intensely." It is used elsewhere in certain stories in the Gospels to imply a deep, affectionate, reverential worship of Jesus. That Judas betrayed the guileless Son of God while pretending deep and earnest affection for him makes Judas's deed all the more despicable.

The Arrest and the Temple Connection

The composition of the group that came to arrest Jesus is significant. Luke indicates the mob included "the chief priests, and captains of the temple, and the elders" (Luke 22:52)—all associated with the Temple. The chief priests preserved spiritual order by performing the ordinances of Aaronic Priesthood temple worship (the Temple at Jerusalem was not a Melchizedek Priesthood temple), the captains of the Temple kept physical order on the Temple Mount, and the elders were spiritual and social leaders who taught in the Temple. Some scholars have even suggested that the elders came from the ranks of the priests, who, of course, had responsibility to serve in the Temple. (The term *elder* in Judaism of the first century after Christ is not to be confused with the Melchizedek Priesthood office.) The "captains of the temple" were officials known from Old Testament times.

The arresting party was essentially the same group of conspirators responsible for planning the seizure and execution, indeed the premeditated murder, of Jesus just a couple of days earlier, as Matthew had reported:

> And it came to pass, when Jesus had finished all
> these sayings, he said unto his disciples,

Ye know that after two days is the feast of the passover, and the Son of man is betrayed to be crucified.

Then assembled together the chief priests, and the scribes, and the elders of the people, unto the palace of the high priest, who was called Caiaphas,

And consulted that they might take Jesus by subtilty, and kill him. (Matthew 26:1–4; Mark 14:1)

Additionally, Luke comments that "the captains" of the Temple were among Judas's initial contacts with whom he worked out the details of the betrayal and, thus, were among the conspirators (Luke 22:4).

The irony is that the Temple was supposed to be the house of the Lord, meaning the home of both our Father in Heaven and his Son Jesus Christ. At the first cleansing of the Temple, at the beginning of his ministry, Jesus had referred to the Temple as "my Father's house" (John 2:16). And at the second cleansing, at the end of his ministry, he had referred to the Temple as "my house" (Matthew 21:13). The Temple was supposed to be the place of supreme sanctity. In reality it had become the habitation of the wicked. Little wonder that when Jesus uttered his last lament over Jerusalem just a couple of days before his arrest, he implied that the Divine Presence had altogether abandoned the Temple structure: "Behold, *your* house is left unto *you* desolate" (Matthew 23:38; emphasis added). Because those responsible for the care of the Temple were also responsible for the Savior's premeditated murder, the Temple was ripe for destruction. That destruction came a few decades later (A.D. 70) at the hands of the very Romans who helped with the arrest and execution of the Lord.

The Gospel of John implies that the arresting band contained

17

Roman soldiers as well. The word *band* in the King James Version (John 18:3) is translated from the Greek word for *cohort,* a subdivision of the Roman army. Presumably, Roman leadership at some level was persuaded to help with the arrest, though they probably were not in on the actual conspiracy to take Jesus' life. Having Roman soldiers in the group of Temple officers who went to arrest Jesus would have given Jewish leaders and conspirators the cloak of official business and government power to hide behind. They feared the Savior's power and his popularity with the people. Mark makes this clear: "And the scribes and chief priests heard it, and sought how they might destroy him: for they feared him, because all the people was astonished at his doctrine" (Mark 11:18). Thus, the conspirators insisted that the arrest not take place during the feast of the Passover in order to avoid a possible riot (Matthew 26:4–5). Luke adds that they extracted a promise from Judas that he would betray Jesus "in the absence of the multitude" (Luke 22:6).

PETER AND THE HIGH PRIEST'S SERVANT

All of the Gospels report that as Jesus was being arrested, a scuffle ensued. The chief apostle was at the center of it. Peter showed no hesitation in defending the life of his Master by force in the face of overwhelming odds, though only the Gospel of John mentions Peter by name. He drew his short sword, the kind Galilean fishermen used, and cut off the ear of Malchus, the servant of the high priest (John 18:10). That action, in turn, drew a stern rebuke from the Savior to put away the sword. Those who live by the sword are destined to die by the sword, and Jesus did not want anything to happen to his chief apostle, the future earthly head of the Church.

In fact, Jesus likely averted combat between the apostles and the armed mob with a comment he had made earlier, in the upper room. When trying to teach his apostles that he would shortly be arrested, tried, and "reckoned among the transgressors," and that they needed to be prepared for what lay ahead, the apostles misunderstood the kind of preparation he meant, and they said, "Lord, behold, here are two swords." Jesus answered, "It is enough," meaning, that was enough of such foolish talk (Luke 22:37–38). Had the apostles tried to arm themselves more fully, a real blood bath might have ensued at the arrest of Jesus. As it was, Judas's kiss, combined with the mob's initial overtures to arrest Jesus, evoked from the apostles a question about whether or not to retaliate: "Lord, shall we smite with the sword?" (Luke 22:49). Before Jesus could respond, Peter acted out his misplaced determination to defend his Master.

In rebuking Peter for his attack on Malchus, Jesus asked if Peter didn't realize that he could immediately summon more than twelve legions of angels from God the Father to defend himself? (Matthew 26:53). In first-century Roman Judea, the chief subdivision of the imperial army was a legion, a unit composed of up to six thousand foot soldiers, plus cavalry. What an army of angelic warriors that would have been! Twelve legions of angels—seventy-two thousand heavenly warriors with incomprehensible power at their disposal. It will be remembered that one angel of the Lord in a single night slew 185,000 Assyrian warriors when they threatened the city of Jerusalem in 701 B.C. (2 Kings 19:35). The people in Jesus' day knew very well the structure and power of the Roman military, and such an image would not have been lost on any who heard the Savior's question that night.

The Savior's rebuke of Peter included a reminder to all the other apostles that the ordeal of the bitter cup was not yet finished and that the remaining ordeal was the Father's will. Jesus asked them, "The cup which my Father hath given me, shall I not drink it?" (John 18:11). Certainly the Savior had unlimited power at his disposal. But his purpose that night was to bless, not to destroy. He was now unalterably committed to carry out the supreme saving mission of the Father and thus fulfill the scriptures. He was loyal to the Father at all costs.

Peter's seemingly impulsive action adds yet another confirming witness to our understanding of the chief apostle's unwavering sense of loyalty. His action against Malchus is in perfect harmony with the consistent portrayal in the Gospels of a chief apostle who acted fearlessly to keep Jesus out of harm's way by any means at his disposal. Malchus could very well have been a high-ranking servant of the high priest because he was in the front of the mob, leading the enforcement of the Temple conspirators' wishes. It is likely that Peter was aiming not for Malchus's ear but rather his head and that Malchus was fortunate to lose only his ear by means of deft maneuvering. Remarkably, Jesus healed the man's ear on the spot, but even that miraculous act apparently gave no one pause to consider who it was they were arresting (Luke 22:51). This is another of the great ironies of this whole drama that demonstrate, again and again, the unsurpassed character and meekness of the Master. Poise in the face of provocation, concern for others despite personal tribulation and hardship—these are characteristics of the kind of meekness the Savior displayed, and these characteristics are a true measure of just how closely we mirror Christlike behavior in our own lives.

The healing of Malchus's ear is the last of the Savior's

recorded miracles in mortality, before the occurrence of the greatest miracle of all time: the Resurrection. It seems significant that only Luke—the physician interested in physiological matters, the disciple whose Gospel contains the only biblical description of the Savior's bloody sweat in Gethsemane, the writer who preserves the account of the Savior's compassionate act of raising the widow's son from death—he alone describes the healing of Malchus by the mortal Son of God, who was experiencing his own greatest distress. From this account we see again Luke's interest in the workings of the physical body and, even more, in the Savior's unwavering compassion, which are hallmarks of his Gospel record.

Then said Jesus unto him, Put up again thy sword into his place: for all they that take the sword shall perish with the sword.

Thinkest thou that I cannot now pray to my Father, and he shall presently give me more than twelve legions of angels?

But how then shall the scriptures be fulfilled, that thus it must be?

In that same hour said Jesus to the multitudes, Are ye come out as against a thief with swords and staves for to take me? I sat daily with you teaching in the temple, and ye laid no hold on me.

But all this was done, that the scriptures of the prophets might be fulfilled. Then all the disciples forsook him, and fled.

MATTHEW 26:52–56

Then the band and the captain and officers of the Jews took Jesus, and bound him.

JOHN 18:12

And there followed him a certain young man, having a linen cloth cast about his naked body; and the young men laid hold on him:
And he left the linen cloth, and fled from them naked.

MARK 14:51–52

CHAPTER 2

Prophecy Fulfilled in the Arrest

With the miracle of healing accomplished and Malchus made whole, Jesus was seized by the police force and "led away with a rope around his neck, as a common criminal, to be judged by the arch-criminals who as Jews sat in Aaron's seat" (McConkie, "Purifying Power of Gethsemane," 9). Of all those who have written about Jesus' arrest, Elder Bruce R. McConkie alone describes a rope around the Savior's neck, an insight that cannot be ascribed to anything other than the visionary gift of a modern apostolic witness.

The irony, the contradiction inherent in this situation, is overwhelming: arch-criminals judging the Sinless One, who was forced to play the role of a base criminal. With a noose around his neck, Jesus fulfilled the symbolism of the scapegoat in the Israelite sacrificial system—the animal upon whose head the sins of the people were laid on the Day of Atonement and who was led away to be released into the wilderness to perish bearing those sins (Leviticus 16:21–22).

JESUS AND ISAAC

Jesus' arrest and seizure fulfilled Old Testament symbolism in another powerful way. John tells us that "the band and the captain and officers of the Jews took Jesus, and *bound* him" (John 18:12; emphasis added). The perfect foreshadowing of the Master's binding was the binding of Isaac by Abraham, or what the Jews call the *Akedah*, the Binding of Isaac. "And they came to the place which God had told him of; and Abraham built an altar there, and laid the wood in order, and bound Isaac his son, and laid him on the altar upon the wood" (Genesis 22:9). Just as Isaac meekly submitted to God's will and his father's intent to offer him as a sacrifice, so too Jesus meekly submitted to God's will and his Father's intent to offer him as the great and last sacrifice in order to bring salvation to those who believe on his name (Alma 34:14–15).

Undoubtedly that is why the Book of Mormon prophet Jacob taught that "it was accounted unto Abraham in the wilderness to be obedient unto the commands of God in offering up his son Isaac, which is a similitude of God and his Only Begotten Son" (Jacob 4:5). Not only did the binding of Isaac point to and correspond with the binding of Jesus but the general locations where each event occurred pointed to and corresponded with each other. Perhaps that is the reason God commanded Abraham to go to Moriah for the sacrifice of Isaac. What happened to Isaac and where it happened foreshadowed the very thing that would happen to Jesus and where it would happen to him, as Abraham himself came to understand: "And Abraham called the name of that place Jehovah-jireh [literally, "Jehovah will be seen"]: as it is said to this day, In the mount of the Lord it shall be seen" [or, "In a mount the Lord shall be manifest"] (Genesis 22:14). The Savior would be seen in the place where Isaac once was.

Jewish teachings about the *Akedah,* or the Binding of Isaac, speak of the "ashes of Isaac," as though Abraham had actually completed the sacrifice because Abraham's unwavering intention was to complete it. In other words, God regarded the intent of Abraham's heart to follow through with the sacrifice the same as if he had actually sacrificed Isaac. This principle is both noble and true. God judges us not only by our actions but by the righteous desires of our hearts (D&C 137:9). That is very good news, because sometimes our desires turn out to be much nobler than our actions. As Christians we believe that Abraham could possess that kind of single-minded intent to go through with the sacrifice of his son because of his faith in God's power "to raise him up, even from the dead" (Hebrews 11:19). Thus, Abraham's sacrifice of Isaac is also tied to the Resurrection and to his prophetic belief in it. Furthermore, the King James Version of the Bible emphasizes the parallel between the sacrifice of Jesus and the sacrifice of Isaac by referring to Isaac as Abraham's only begotten son, in similitude of God's Only Begotten Son: "By faith Abraham, when he was tried, offered up Isaac: and he that had received the promises offered up his only begotten son" (Hebrews 11:17). Jesus and Isaac are the only two beings in the King James Version of the Bible to whom the title "only begotten son" is applied.

But for Latter-day Saints there is another, even more remarkable, dimension of Abraham's sacrifice that makes his story much more than just a theological parallel to, or literary foreshadowing of, the sacrifice of Jesus Christ. Each one of us is called by the Savior to participate in the kind of sacrifice made by Abraham and, therefore, made by the Savior. The Savior declared to the Prophet Joseph Smith through revelation: "Therefore, they must needs be chastened and tried, even as Abraham, who was commanded to offer up his only son. For all those who will not endure chastening, but deny me, cannot be sanctified" (D&C 101:4–5). Of Abraham's sacrifice and God's requirement that each of us pass through the same experience, the Prophet Joseph further said, "The sacrifice required of Abraham in the offering up of Isaac, shows that if a man would attain to the keys of the kingdom of an endless life; he must sacrifice all things" (*Teachings of the Prophet Joseph Smith*, 322).

None of us knows when or what kind of Abrahamic tests we will pass through. But we may take heart in knowing that our experience actually parallels the experience of both Abraham and the Lord Jesus Christ. God is not only mindful of us in our trials but will aid us because he wants to exalt us. Like the Savior, we will triumph over all our foes (D&C 121:8), including the most menacing ones: sin, death, sorrow, and heartache. The binding of Isaac and the binding of Jesus teach profound lessons about the meekness to submit and the character to endure. Perhaps at some point in our lives we may feel bound by circumstances beyond our control. If we submit patiently and endure faithfully, we will receive the blessings of Abraham and the Savior—all that the Father himself possesses—so that as it was said of Abraham and Isaac, so it will be said of us: "They have entered into their exaltation, according to the promises, and sit upon thrones, and are not angels but are gods" (D&C 132:37).

President John Taylor once said that the Prophet Joseph Smith taught that eternal life cannot be gained in any other way except by being tried and proven as was Abraham but that in the testing comes a closeness to God that cannot be enjoyed in any other way: "You will have all kinds of trials to pass through. And it is quite as necessary for you to be tried as it was for Abraham and other men of God. . . . God will feel after you, and He will take hold of you and wrench your very heart strings, and if you cannot stand it, you will not be fit for an inheritance in the Celestial Kingdom of God" (*Journal of Discourses*, 24:197).

ONE FINAL QUESTION

Standing helplessly by, as Jesus was about to be led away from Gethsemane in bondage, the disciples heard their Master ask one final, penetrating question. It pointedly reminded all those present of the connection between the members of the mob and their leadership roles in the Jerusalem Temple:

> Then Jesus said unto the chief priests, and captains of the temple, and the elders, which were come to him, Be ye come out, as against a thief, with swords and staves?
>
> When I was daily with you in the temple, ye stretched forth no hands against me: but this is your hour, and the power of darkness. (Luke 22:52–53; Matthew 26:55; Mark 14:48–49)

In one stroke, Jesus emphasized to his captors their hypocrisy as well as their depravity. He was saying, in effect, "You were in the Temple every day, in that holiest of places. I was also there, yet you didn't have the courage to arrest me openly, while I was teaching in your midst. Instead, you have come after me as though I were a thief in the night, precisely because *you* are the ones ruled by the power of darkness." The

27

Greek original of the last clause of Luke 22:53 is actually stronger than the translation in the King James Version and might be rendered: "But this is your hour and the authority of darkness." Jesus left no doubt in the minds of the chief priest and captains of the Temple that he knew they were operating under the authority of Satan, the prince of darkness. Again, we see in Jesus remarkable teaching skills: boldness, thorough knowledge of his audience, and precision of language. We are reminded of what others have said about great teachers: They teach their audiences what they need to hear, not what they want to hear.

THE DISCIPLES FLED

At this point, Matthew's record links the arrest and seizure of Jesus with the fulfillment of prophecy: "But all this was done, that the scriptures might be fulfilled" (Matthew 26:56). Then there immediately follows the wrenching declaration that as Jesus was being led away, "all the disciples forsook him, and fled" (Matthew 26:56; Mark 14:50). The Savior of the world was abandoned by his closest friends. Here the heart of every modern disciple goes out to him, because most of us know in some small measure the feelings that come from being left alone. Though it is tempting to view this situation in its harshest light, regarding it as an example of supreme disloyalty, it appears that there were mitigating circumstances and that we should temper our judgment of the eleven special witnesses.

First of all, as Elder James E. Talmage observed, once the armed police force showed up, resistance to the arrest of Jesus was useless. He also noted that the apostles were in real jeopardy themselves:

The eleven apostles, seeing that resistance was useless, not only on account of disparity of numbers and supply of weapons but chiefly because of Christ's determination to submit, turned and fled. . . . That they were really in jeopardy is shown by an incident preserved by Mark alone. An unnamed young man, aroused from sleep by the tumult of the marching band, had sallied forth with no outer covering but a linen sheet. His interest in the arrest of Jesus and his close approach caused some of the guardsmen or soldiers to seize him; but he broke loose and escaped leaving the sheet in their hands. (*Jesus the Christ*, 617)

This story of the young man fleeing is one of the strangest in the Gospels; it is presented only in Mark 14:51–52. It cannot be referring to one of the apostles because they had all fled, and we know nothing else about it from scripture; however, an apocryphal document called *The Secret Gospel of Mark*, which claims to be a fuller account of Mark's Gospel, indicates that the man in the linen cloth was a disciple of the Master who had come to Gethsemane to receive from the Savior special teachings related to the mysteries of the kingdom. Such an idea resonates with Latter-day Saints because of its obvious connection to temple ordinances. And such a concept about Jesus initiating his disciples into the mysteries of the kingdom is substantiated in the writings and traditions of the early Church, including the apocryphal Acts of John and Eusebius's *History of the Church*. Be that as it may, we do not know the identity of the young man in Mark's story, though one tradition holds that it was Mark himself.

A second reason for tempering our view toward the fleeing

apostles that awful night comes from the testimony of John the Beloved. He takes pains to report in different portions of his Gospel how protective Jesus was of his apostles, perhaps even to the point of suggesting or encouraging their flight or dispersal from the garden, because he did not want any harm to come to them. For example, from the Savior's great high priestly prayer, we read this petition on behalf of the apostles:

> I pray for them: I pray not for the world, but for them which thou hast given me; for they are thine. . . .
>
> And now I am no more in the world, but these are in the world, and I come to thee. Holy Father, keep through thine own name those whom thou hast given me, that they may be one, as we are. . . .
>
> I have given them thy word; and the world hath hated them, because they are not of the world, even as I am not of the world.
>
> I pray not that thou shouldest take them out of the world, but that thou shouldest keep them from the evil. (John 17:9, 11, 14–15)

Finally, the Savior tried to protect his apostles and ensure their safety at the moment he was being arrested by the mob. "Then asked he them again, Whom seek ye? And they said, Jesus of Nazareth. Jesus answered, I have told you that I am he: if therefore ye seek me, let these go their way: That the saying might be fulfilled, which he spake, Of them which thou gavest me have I lost none" (John 18:7–9).

Given all we know about the dangers ready to befall the apostles at the time of Jesus' arrest, perhaps it is more instructive to think of the episode of their fleeing as a scattering caused by external forces. This seems to be the sense in which the prophet Zechariah prophesied of the event: "Awake, O sword, against my shepherd, and against the man that is my fellow, saith the Lord of hosts: smite the shepherd, and the sheep shall be scattered: and I will turn mine hand upon the little ones" (Zechariah 13:7). Certainly the Good Shepherd was struck or smitten, the sheep scattered, and the hand of the smiter turned against the little ones, or apostles.

There is no question that Jesus knew beforehand and foretold these events affecting the apostles, including the prophecy of Zechariah. When Jesus and the Quorum of the Twelve finished the Last Supper, Mark records: "And when they had sung an hymn, they went out into the mount of Olives. And Jesus saith unto them, All ye shall be offended because of me this night: for it is written, I will smite the shepherd, and the sheep shall be scattered. But after that I am risen, I will go before you into Galilee" (Mark 14:26–28). Let me emphasize that even though the apostles would be scattered, Jesus ends this prophecy on a note of optimism, saying, in effect, "Even though you're going to be scattered, we will meet again in Galilee after I am resurrected."

With the scattering of the apostles as their Master was being arrested, the die was cast. Prophecy was fulfilled. Irrevocable forces were set in motion. There was no turning back from the final events of the Savior's remaining ordeal—from the final swallows of the bitter cup.

And led him away to Annas first; for he was father in law to Caiaphas, which was the high priest that same year.

The high priest then asked Jesus of his disciples, and of his doctrine.

Jesus answered him, I spake openly to the world; I ever taught in the synagogue, and in the temple, whither the Jews always resort; and in secret have I said nothing.

Why askest thou me? ask them which heard me, what I have said unto them: behold, they know what I said.

And when he had thus spoken, one of the officers which stood by struck Jesus with the palm of his hand, saying, Answerest thou the high priest so?

Jesus answered him, If I have spoken evil, bear witness of the evil: but if well, why smitest thou me?

Now Annas had sent him bound unto Caiaphas the high priest.

JOHN 18:13, 19–24

Now the chief priests, and elders, and all the council, sought false witness against Jesus, to put him to death.

. . . at the last came two false witnesses,

And said, This fellow said, I am able to destroy the temple of God, and to build it in three days.

MATTHEW 26:59–61

CHAPTER 3

Arraignment before the High Priests

In the dark hours of the night or the early morning, Jesus was marched away from Gethsemane under armed guard to be interrogated by Caiaphas, the high priest who held judicial power over the Jewish people and ruled at the pleasure of Roman authorities. John tells us, however, that Jesus was first taken to a man named Annas, father-in-law to Caiaphas (John 18:13).

ANNAS, THE POWER BROKER

Annas wielded great influence and seems to have been the real power operating behind the scenes. He himself had ruled as high priest during the days of Jesus' youth (A.D. 7–15) but had been deposed by the Romans, though he was still referred to by the title high priest (John 18:19, 22), much as Latter-day Saints often continue to refer to a man as bishop even though he is not currently officiating in the office. That Annas remained a person of tremendous influence in the Sanhedrin is attested by the fact that his son-in-law, five of his sons, and a grandson became high priest. It seems reasonable to assume that when Annas gave his approval of an action, it was carried out.

Standing before Annas, Jesus was in dreadful physical condition. By this time the Savior had already been awake for an entire day and night. He had experienced the bloody agony in Gethsemane and been forced to cross the Kidron Valley, marching up its steep western slope to the residence of Annas on the western hill of Jerusalem where the wealthy and powerful lived. Ancient stone steps still mark the likely path. Jesus stood before Annas in bloody garments. He was suffering from severe emotional and mental trauma, loss of blood, shock brought on by loss of fluids from his body, and chills from the cold night air passing over his damp body (blood mixed with sweat). Such physiological distress would have caused collapse in most mortals. But the Savior's physical ordeal was far from over in those early morning hours of what the Christian world calls Good Friday.

Responding to Annas's inquiries about his doctrine, Jesus indicated that everything he had said and done was an open record seen and heard by the Jews in their synagogues and their Temple in Jerusalem (John 18:20). It should be remembered that when he was arrested, he had also proclaimed that he had "sat daily . . . teaching in the temple" (Matthew 26:55). Jesus suggested to Annas that he personally ask those who had heard Jesus teach just what the nature of His doctrine was all about (John 18:21). This suggestion was intended to keep fresh in the minds of Annas and the others associated with the interrogation the link between Jesus, the Temple, and all those who were responsible for the Savior's arrest and later crucifixion. In one way or another, everyone associated with the conspiracy to kill Jesus was connected to the Temple. Remember, Matthew identifies the *planners* of the plot as the chief priests, scribes, and elders of the people, who served or taught in the Temple (Matthew 26:3–5). And Luke describes those sent to *arrest* Jesus as "the chief priests, and captains of the temple, and the elders" (Luke 22:52).

The uncomfortably direct connection Jesus pointed out between Temple and conspirators did not go unnoticed. For his comments Jesus received the first of several abusive slaps in the face, intended both to humiliate and to inflict physical pain. Perhaps it was retaliation for the high priest's own embarrassment. Slaves and servants in hellenistic society were liable to being buffeted by slaps with the open hand.

Jesus knew that Annas knew that He had spoken the truth and asked the high priest to produce evidence to the contrary (John 18:23). But Annas chose to further the predetermined, premeditated aims of the conspirators to get rid of Jesus "by craft" (Mark 14:1). He therefore "sent [Jesus] bound unto Caiaphas the high priest" (John 18:24). Though the tone of John's comment implies a separate location for the next phase of Jesus' arraignment before the Jews, it has been suggested that the residences of Annas and Caiaphas shared a common courtyard, the place where Peter awaited his Master's fate (Matthew 26:69). It is also important to note that this is the second mention of the binding of Jesus in John's Gospel. John must have been deeply affected by the Savior's having been shackled.

BEFORE CAIAPHAS AND THE COUNCIL

In the early morning hours of the most fateful Friday the universe has ever known, the chief priests and scribes came together to judge Jesus in their council meeting (Matthew 26:59). The high priest was in charge (Matthew 26:62–66).

Caiaphas, or Joseph ben Caiaphas, served as high priest from A.D. 18 to A.D. 36. The high priest during Old Testament times was the primary official of the Israelite religious system. After the Exile (586–538 B.C.) and the construction of Zerubbabel's Temple, or the Second Temple (520–515 B.C.), the high priest became the supreme authority in Judaism, acquiring, generally speaking, the prestige and power formerly held by the Israelite kings. During the period of Maccabean consolidation, from about 141 to 63 B.C., the high priest was the unquestioned religious and political head of the independent nation of Israel.

With the coming of Roman overlordship in 63 B.C., the high priests were appointed and deposed at the pleasure of the Romans. Herod the Great, vassal king in the land of Israel (37–4 B.C.), diminished the high priestly office to almost nothing. But after his death, the Roman procurators, or governors, gave the office of high priest greater power in local affairs and strengthened its prestige considerably, especially with the pro-Roman family of Annas and Caiaphas. This close connection between the Roman rulers and the high priestly office made the family of its holders, including Annas, Caiaphas, and their successors, very suspicious of anyone who seemed to oppose Roman rule or who was likely to upset the status quo.

The Gospel of John confirms the general picture of Caiaphas and other Jewish leaders as being far more concerned with keeping peace with the Romans by getting rid of Jesus than with the righteousness of their nation or the recognized identity of the Messiah. "If we let him thus alone, all men will believe on him: and the Romans shall come and take away both our place and nation" (John 11:48; see also vv. 47–51). In addition, they sought to destroy the undeniable evidence of Jesus' great power by killing Lazarus. The raising of Lazarus from the dead had been the final straw, so to speak, in Jesus' actions. The leaders became unalterably motivated to get rid of both the prophet from Galilee and his friend Lazarus. "Much people of the Jews therefore knew that he was there: and they came not for Jesus' sake only, but that they might see Lazarus also, whom he had raised from the dead. But the chief priests consulted that they might put Lazarus also to death; Because that by reason of him many of the Jews went away, and believed on Jesus" (John 12:9–11). It seems that the wickedness of the chief priests knew no bounds. They were consummately evil men.

There also seems to have been another reason behind the determination to eliminate Jesus: he had interfered with economic traffic on the Temple Mount (John 2:14–16; Matthew 21:12–13). The high priestly family was in charge of such commerce and had grown wealthier because of it. They saw it as a necessary (and welcome) part of activities at the house of the Lord. But Jesus had called all of this into question when he referred to the Temple as a house of merchandise and a den of thieves (John 2:16; Matthew 21:13). The Gospel of Mark makes the direct connection between Jesus' actions in this regard and the culmination of plots to take his life: "And he taught, saying unto them, Is it not written, My house shall be called of all nations the house of prayer? but ye have made it a den of thieves. And the scribes and chief priests heard it, and sought how they might destroy him" (Mark 11:17–18).

It is no small thing to say that economic issues were at the heart of the conspiracy to murder Jesus. From nearly the dawn of creation on this earth, getting gain has been one of the foundation stones of wickedness, if not the cornerstone itself. Cain, who slew his brother Abel over such matters, entered into a covenant with Satan to promote this activity. "And Cain said:

Truly I am Mahan, the master of this great secret, that I may murder and get gain. Wherefore Cain was called Master Mahan, and he gloried in his wickedness" (Moses 5:31). Murder to get gain! This is still a moving force in the world today. Wars have been fought because of it. Nations have fallen due to it. Untold individual human misery has resulted from it.

Is it any wonder then that when God himself came to earth as a mortal, and the great forces of righteousness and wickedness did battle face to face, he would ultimately confront the "great secret," the Mahanic principle, and lose his life over it?

WHICH COUNCIL?

It is impossible to know exactly which group of Jewish leaders, led by Caiaphas, interrogated Jesus after his examination by Annas. In the New Testament the Greek word *synedrion*, "Sanhedrin," is used for judicial courts in general and is sometimes conflated with *presbyterion*, "council of elders." Theoretically, the high priest presided over the supreme judicial and legislative court in Jerusalem, called the Great Sanhedrin. It had seventy-one members and met in the Chamber of Hewn Stone in the Temple complex. Our information about this council, however, comes in part from the later codification of Jewish oral law and tradition called the Mishnah (ca. A.D. 200). We do not know whether this information about the Great Sanhedrin and associated legal regulations reflects third-century practice, or Second Temple reality, or an idealized conceptualization projected back from the third century to the first century, or a combination of these.

Additionally, in the Mishnah, the word *Sanhedrin* is also used for law courts of twenty-three members that decided capital cases. Was the council before whom Jesus stood this

lesser Sanhedrin? To further complicate matters, the Jewish historian Josephus (born A.D. 37) speaks of many local and national
councils (*synedria*, or Sanhedrins) whose powers and composition changed with political circumstances. Therefore, we con-
clude with Elder James E. Talmage that the size of the judicial
body involved in Jesus' arraignment is uncertain and of small
importance compared to the monumental nature of the whole
atoning act (*Jesus the Christ*, 623).

One thing is certain, however, and that is that Jesus'
arraignment before Caiaphas and the other Jewish authorities
was neither legal nor fair. Perhaps the most sinister aspect of the
whole business is best reported by Matthew: "Now the chief
priests, and elders, and *all* the council, sought false witness
against Jesus, to put him to death; but found none: yea though
many false witnesses came, yet found they none" (Matthew
26:59–60; emphasis added; see also Mark 14:55). Thus, we are
also sure that the Jewish council that morning could not have
been made up of the full complement of seventy-one San-
hedrists because, as Matthew and Mark testify, the whole council present that morning was guilty of suborning perjury and at
least two members of the Sanhedrin, Joseph of Arimathaea and
Nicodemus, were righteous men who were not associated with
the conspiracy. Nicodemus defended the Savior during his ministry (John 7:50–53), and Joseph of Arimathaea was "a rich and
faithful Israelite who took no part in the condemnation of our
Lord" (LDS Bible Dictionary, 717). These two men were later
involved in the burial of their Master.

Deuteronomy 17:6 states, "At the mouth of two witnesses,
or three witnesses, shall he that is worthy of death be put
to death; but at the mouth of one witness he shall not be put to
death." That *all* the council would scrupulously adhere to this

law of witnesses as outlined in the law of Moses by seeking more than one witness but then wholeheartedly endorse false witnesses and the suborning of perjury is testimony enough to the thorough and murderous corruption of Jewish leadership in Jerusalem at the time. These hypocrites would not dare violate the outward forms of the law for fear of the people, but they had no qualms about secretly manipulating, even destroying, the moral underpinnings of their society in order to ensure the fulfillment of their plan of premeditated murder. Elder Talmage comments:

> In the Sanhedrin, every member was a judge; the judicial body was to hear the testimony, and, according to that testimony and nought else, render a decision on every case duly presented. . . . But in the so-called trial of Jesus, the judges not only sought witnesses, but specifically tried to find false witnesses. Though many false witnesses came, yet there was no 'witness' or testimony against the Prisoner, for the suborned perjurers failed to agree among themselves; and even the lawless Sanhedrists hesitated to openly violate the fundamental requirement that at least two concordant witnesses must testify against an accused person, for, otherwise, the case had to be dismissed. (*Jesus the Christ*, 623)

Surely this is one of the moments the Lord had in mind anciently when he spoke with Enoch the seer about the inhabitants of this earth: "Wherefore, I can stretch forth mine hands and hold all the creations which I have made; and mine eye can pierce them also, and among all the workmanship of mine hands there has not been so great wickedness as among thy brethren" (Moses 7:36). The Savior's arraignment before Jewish leaders must also have been part of Jacob's visionary understanding when he said: "Wherefore, as I said unto you, it must needs be expedient that Christ—for in the last night the angel spake unto me that this should be his name—should come among the Jews, among those who are the more wicked part of the world; and they shall crucify him—for thus it behooveth our God, and there is none other nation on earth that would crucify their God" (2 Nephi 10:3).

THE SAVIOR'S CRIME

At last the Jewish leaders produced two false witnesses, though their respective testimonies did not agree with one another in details (Mark 14:59). The strength of the warning against false witnesses in the Mosaic law helps us to understand just how badly these leaders wanted Jesus eliminated. Perjurers were liable to the same punishment intended for the accused (Deuteronomy 19:16–19). Ultimately, the accusation against Jesus centered on the Jerusalem Temple: "And there arose certain, and bare false witness against him, saying, We heard him say, I will destroy this temple that is made with hands, and within three days I will build another made without hands" (Mark 14:57–58).

The exact nature of the crime here is difficult to ferret out. Elder Talmage sees this initial accusation as focusing on sedition: "The plan of the conspiring rulers appears to have been that of convicting Christ on a charge of sedition, making Him out to be a dangerous disturber of the nation's peace, an assailant of established institutions, and consequently an inciter of opposition against the vassal autonomy of the Jewish nation, and the supreme dominion of Rome" (*Jesus the Christ*, 624–25). This interpretation accords well with the later scene reported by Luke, in which the charge that was leveled against Jesus by "the whole multitude of them that arose and led him unto Pilate" was officially registered as "perverting the nation" (Luke 23:1–2).

The flurry of activity occurring immediately after the accusation by the false witnesses helps us to see that the charge of sedition, which would lead to Jesus' conviction by the Romans, was coupled with blasphemy, the high crime in Jewish society, which would ensure Jesus' conviction among the Jews. Matthew's account tells us what happened after the perjured testimony had been accepted:

> And the high priest arose, and said unto him, Answerest thou nothing? what is it which these witness against thee?
>
> But Jesus held his peace. And the high priest answered and said unto him, I adjure thee by the living God, that thou tell us whether thou be the Christ, the Son of God.
>
> Jesus saith unto him, Thou hast said: nevertheless I say unto you, Hereafter shall ye see the Son of man sitting on the right hand of power, and coming in the clouds of heaven.
>
> Then the high priest rent his clothes, saying, He hath spoken blasphemy; what further need have we of witnesses? behold, now ye have heard his blasphemy.
>
> What think ye? They answered and said, He is guilty of death. (Matthew 26:62–66)

Throughout this pretense of a proper hearing, Jesus stood before his accusers calm and quiet, refraining from comment on the scurrilous charges (Matthew 26:63). In those moments of silence, Isaiah's unparalleled messianic prophecy was fulfilled: "He was oppressed, and he was afflicted, yet he opened not his mouth: he is brought as a lamb to the slaughter, and as a sheep before her shearers is dumb, so he openeth not his mouth" (Isaiah 53:7). In an action reminiscent of high courtroom drama, Caiaphas then arose from his seat and forced Jesus to respond to his interrogation by placing him under oath, "I adjure thee by the living God, that thou tell us whether thou be the Christ, the Son of God" (Matthew 26:63). There is something disturbing in the vehement tone that comes through the written words of Matthew's text. We also note that Caiaphas seems to have equated the title "Christ" (Messiah) with the title "Son of God" (v. 63). Here the Gospel of Mark uses "Son of the Blessed" instead of the more jarring "Son of God." In responding to the high priest's direct question about his identity, Jesus again left no room for doubt. As he did when he was arrested, Jesus identified himself by using the divine name "I am" (Mark 14:62). "It was an unqualified avowal of divine parentage, and inherent Godship," wrote Elder Talmage (*Jesus the Christ*, 626). In this Jesus was guilty of nothing except telling the truth.

Caiaphas tore his clothes when he heard Jesus answer. Likely, from the high priest's perspective, this was the hoped-for self-incrimination. The tearing of one's clothing anciently was done to convey shock, outrage, or grief—and to signify the death of a member of one's family or community (Genesis 37:34; Numbers 14:6; 2 Samuel 1:11). Perhaps Caiaphas did it to register his outrage dramatically, pretended though it was, and to signal Jesus' death as a foregone conclusion. Yet, the high priest was not supposed to tear his clothes, according to divine rules for priestly behavior (Leviticus 21:10). He was now the one who was actually guilty of breaking the laws of God—not Jesus—but he and his associates had the pretext they needed to move forward with their premeditated plan of murder. With only a few more words, Caiaphas forestalled any verdict other than guilty: "He hath spoken blasphemy; what further need have we of witnesses? . . . What think ye?" (Matthew 26:65–66). To Caiaphas's carefully orchestrated manipulations, the entire council responded, "He is guilty of death" (v. 66).

These final irregularities encapsulate the entire proceedings. The members of the Sanhedrin, judges of Israel, were supposed to vote on the verdict one by one, yet they spoke in unison. More important, a unanimous verdict of guilt pronounced on the same day as the trial constituted an automatic acquittal and the defendant was supposed to be set free (Mishna Sanhedrin 4:1). Why? Because such proceedings, according to ancient rabbinic law, smacked of collusion. "If you're tried and everybody in the room is against you, then there must be a conspiracy, because that many people can't all agree on one thing" (Kofford, "Trial of Christ," 15). Ironically, the very thing Jewish law was structured to prevent—conspiracy—was the very thing that made the law of no effect in the case of Jesus of Nazareth.

Having accomplished their unwavering goal of convicting Jesus, the council took advantage of the opportunity to vent their anger openly against him whom they regarded as their arch-enemy: the sinless Son of God. Matthew reports that they spat in His face, buffeted (battered) Him, and slapped Him with open palms. Mark and Luke add that they blindfolded Him and then struck Him. This is implied in Matthew's account as well because each of the three Synoptic Gospels indicate that as the members of the council struck Jesus, they also taunted him by commanding him to "prophesy unto us, thou Christ, Who is he that smote thee?" (Matthew 26:68). It is not hard to see the sarcasm dripping from the phrase "thou Christ."

In another of the many powerful ironies of Jesus' situation, Luke tells us that the Jewish council spoke "many other things *blasphemously*" to Jesus (Luke 22:65; emphasis added). The Savior was the one convicted of the charge, but the chief priests were the ones guilty of it.

The Savior of the world bore this horrible abuse with quiet dignity and majesty. Much later the chief apostle testified of his Master's composure in this setting and encouraged us to follow His example: "For even hereunto were ye called: because Christ also suffered for us, leaving us an example, that ye should follow his steps: . . . Who, when he was reviled, reviled not again; when he suffered, he threatened not; but committed himself to him that judgeth righteously" (1 Peter 2:21–23).

Jesus bore his tribulation with patience. He suffered his indignity with dignity. He endured scorn and physical abuse by himself. No one was with him. No man defended him. No one spoke on his behalf. No one protected him. He trod the winepress alone. He was rejected of men, truly "a man of sorrows, and acquainted with grief" (Isaiah 53:3). There is nothing anyone can tell him about loneliness or the unfairness of life. He is able to have perfect empathy for each one of us because he experienced all things, even descended below all things.

Though condemned to death by evil conspirators and premeditating murderers under the most unfair circumstances, the Holy One of Israel willingly surrendered himself in an attitude of perfect meekness. And still the bitter cup was not yet empty.

Now Peter sat without in the palace: and a damsel came unto him, saying, Thou also wast with Jesus of Galilee.

But he denied before them all, saying, I know not what thou sayest.

And when he was gone out into the porch, another maid saw him, and said unto them that were there, This fellow was also with Jesus of Nazareth.

And again he denied with an oath, I do not know the man.

And after a while came unto him they that stood by, and said to Peter, Surely thou also art one of them; for thy speech bewrayeth thee.

Then began he to curse and to swear, saying, I know not the man. And immediately the cock crew.

And Peter remembered the word of Jesus, which said unto him, Before the cock crow, thou shalt deny me thrice. And he went out, and wept bitterly.

MATTHEW 26:69–75

CHAPTER 4

Peter's Denial

At the same time the tragic drama of the Savior's inquisition unfolded inside the palace of the high priest, another drama was being played out outside the palace. There the apostle Peter endured an inquisition of his own.

When the other disciples fled as Jesus was being arrested, Peter followed his Master and the arresting party "afar off unto the high priest's palace" (Matthew 26:58). This palace seems to have housed the residences of both Caiaphas and Annas, before whom Jesus was arraigned first. In keeping with his presentation of unique details, John adds that Peter "followed Jesus, and so did another disciple" who "was known unto the high priest." This disciple went into the palace with Jesus and eventually "spake unto her that kept the door, and brought in Peter" (John 18:15–16). It is not known who this other disciple was, but some scholars have suggested it was John himself.

Given that Matthew and Mark clearly state that at some point Peter "sat without in the palace" (Matthew 26:69), or "Peter was beneath in the palace" (Mark 14:66), it is likely that

Peter was first admitted to Jesus' arraignment before Annas and later sat out in the courtyard while his Master's next hearing, before Caiaphas, took place in another part of the palace complex. This surmise accords well with the archaeological evidence of a courtyard set down the hill below the main palace complex.

The traditional, and probably accurate, location of the high priest's palace is high above the Hinnom Valley on the western hill of Jerusalem, then inside the city walls, and later known as Mount Zion. A fourth-century traveler to Jerusalem, nicknamed the Pilgrim of Bordeaux, said: "In the same valley of Siloam you go up to Mount Sion and you see the site where the house of Caiaphas stood" (*St. Peter "in Gallicantu,"* 2). In the fifth century after Christ, a church was built on this site, and the Crusaders later named it *Gallicantus*, "the cock-crow." In modern times, a dungeon, scourging room, courtyard, artifacts, and a Hebrew inscription have been unearthed on the site that are consistent with expectations associated with the residence and judicial functions of the high priest.

ACCUSATIONS

As Peter sat beside a fire in the palace courtyard, awaiting word regarding the ultimate fate of Jesus, one of the servants of the high priest's household approached him. Mark's account of the scene is similar to that of the other Synoptic Gospels:

> And when she saw Peter warming himself, she looked upon him, and said, And thou also wast with Jesus of Nazareth.
> But he denied, saying, I know not, neither understand

I what thou sayest. And he went out into the porch; and the cock crew.

And a maid saw him again, and began to say to them that stood by, This is one of them.

And he denied it again. And a little after, they that stood by said again to Peter, Surely thou art one of them: for thou art a Galilaean, and thy speech agreeth thereto.

But he began to curse and to swear, saying, I know not this man of whom ye speak.

And the second time the cock crew. And Peter called to mind the word that Jesus said unto him, Before the cock crow twice, thou shalt deny me thrice. And when he thought thereon, he wept. (Mark 14:67–72)

John's account, through shorter, adds an interesting detail:

One of the servants of the high priest, being his kinsman whose ear Peter cut off, saith, Did not I see thee in the garden with him? Peter then denied again: and immediately the cock crew. (John 18:26–27)

Apparently, this kinsman was an eyewitness both to Peter's attack on his relative, Malchus, and to Peter's intimate association with Jesus in the garden.

To fully appreciate the significance of the exchange between Peter and his accusers, we need to go back to events of the Last Supper several hours before. In the upper room the Savior described to his apostles their reaction to events that were about to burst forth upon them: "All ye shall be offended because of me this night." Peter protested, "Though all men shall be offended because of thee, yet will I never be offended" (Matthew 26:31, 33).

Jesus' specific response to Peter teaches us profound lessons, especially in light of the confidence Jesus had in Peter's faithfulness and the potential he knew Peter possessed: "Simon, Simon, behold, Satan hath desired to have you, that he may sift you as wheat: but I have prayed for thee, that thy faith fail not: and when thou art converted, strengthen thy brethren" (Luke 22:31–32).

The thought that any prayer offered by the Savior would not come to pass, nor any prediction of his not be fulfilled, is unthinkable. Peter's faith would not fail, though he had a deeper conversion yet to experience. The texts of all four Gospels indicate that even up to that point, Peter still did not fully comprehend the earth-shaking events soon to overtake the Savior and the early Church. Again the Savior patiently tried to teach Peter of things that must shortly come to pass:

> Simon Peter said unto him, Lord, whither goest thou? Jesus answered him, Whither I go, thou canst not follow me now; but thou shalt follow me afterwards.
>
> Peter said unto him, Lord, why cannot I follow thee now? I will lay down my life for thy sake.
>
> Jesus answered him, Wilt thou lay down thy life for my sake? Verily, verily, I say unto thee, The cock shall not crow, till thou hast denied me thrice. (John 13:36–38)

Peter was never one to shrink from danger, and we cannot doubt that at that moment, and all the moments before it and after it, Peter would have forfeited his life for his Master's. But that was precisely the problem. Peter might recklessly have laid down his life for Jesus when something different was needed and intended by the Savior.

After the Last Supper concluded, events moved along unalterably as the apostles followed Jesus to the Garden of Gethsemane. When the Savior finished praying the same prayer for the third time, the police force of the Jerusalem Temple appeared, ready to arrest Jesus. Peter drew his sword and became embroiled in the events we have already discussed. It important to remember that Peter's selfless act of protection was done in the face of an armed mob who could have easily overwhelmed the chief apostle. That action is in complete harmony with everything else we know about Peter. Even when all the other disciples fled at Jesus' arrest, Peter followed afar off and ended up confronting the two women and the man who accused him of associating with Jesus.

What gives us pause at this point is consideration of Peter's motivation for denying that he knew his Master. Why did he deny Him? The reasons usually given range from fear of personal harm, to weakness, to embarrassment, to pride, to indecision, or to some other flaw or weakness in Peter's character. Yet these reasons seem to contradict everything else we have read about the chief apostle in the New Testament, including his bold, unequivocal confession of the Savior's Sonship at Caesarea Philippi, when a diverse set of opinions regarding Jesus was floating about the land, and his single-minded resolve not to allow anyone to harm the Savior.

In every instance when the impending arrest or death of Jesus had come to Peter's attention, he had been both quick and forceful to say that he would not let such a thing happen (Matthew 16:21–23), and he would protect Jesus at all costs, even at the peril of his own life, which is what happened in Gethsemane when the armed forces of the chief priests could not intimidate a chief apostle who was ready to do battle with all of them (John 18:7–12). Now we are to believe that in the face of a challenge initially put forward by a slave girl, the most unimportant person imaginable in Jewish society, Peter denied even knowing Jesus for fear of being exposed as a follower? (The word *damsel* used in Matthew 26:69 does not convey the lowly position of Peter's first interrogator, but the footnote to that verse in the LDS edition of the Bible approaches it.)

President Spencer W. Kimball's Reflections

Years ago President Spencer W. Kimball invited us to reevaluate our understanding of Peter's actions in a magnificent address entitled *Peter, My Brother*. Speaking of his model and mentor, this modern-day apostle asked penetrating questions: Do we really know Peter's mind and heart? Are we sure of his motives? Do we understand the circumstances of Peter's denial as well as we think we do? President Kimball began his discussion with this admission:

> Some time ago a newspaper in a distant town carried an Easter Sunday religious editorial by a minister who stated that the presiding authority of the early-day church fell because of self-confidence, indecision, evil companions, failure to pray, lack of humility, and fear of man. . . .
>
> As I read this, I had some strange emotions. I was shocked, then I was chilled, then my blood changed its temperature and began to boil. I felt I was attacked viciously, for Peter was my brother, my colleague, my example, my prophet, and God's anointed. I whispered

to myself, "That is not true. He is maligning my brother." (*Peter, My Brother,* 488)

President Kimball discussed the tremendous strength, power, faithfulness, and other apostolic attributes of Peter, including his boldness. Then he said:

> Much of the criticism of Simon Peter is centered in his denial of his acquaintance with the Master. This has been labeled "cowardice." Are we sure of his motive in that recorded denial? He had already given up his occupation and placed all worldly goods on the altar for the cause. . . .
>
> Is it conceivable that the omniscient Lord would give all these powers and keys to one who was a failure or unworthy? . . .
>
> If Peter was frightened in the court when he denied his association with the Lord, how brave he was hours earlier when he drew his sword against an overpowering enemy, the night mob. Later defying the people and state and church officials, he boldly charged, "Him [the Christ] . . . ye have taken, and by wicked hands have crucified and slain." (Acts 2:23.) To the astounded populace at the healing of the cripple at the Gate Beautiful, he exclaimed, "Ye men of Israel . . . the God of our fathers, hath glorified his Son Jesus; whom ye delivered up, and denied him in the presence of Pilate. . . . ye denied the Holy One. . . . And killed the Prince of life, whom God hath raised from the dead; whereof we are witnesses." (Acts 3:12–15.)
>
> Does this portray cowardice? Quite a bold assertion for a timid one. Remember that Peter never denied the

divinity of Christ. He only denied his association or acquaintance with the Christ, which is quite a different matter. . . .

Is it possible that there might have been some other reason for Peter's triple denial? Could he have felt that circumstances justified expediency? When he bore a strong testimony in Caesarea Philippi, he had been told that "they should tell no man that he was Jesus the Christ." (Matthew 16:20.) (*Peter, My Brother*, 488–89)

To what, then, might we attribute Peter's denial? Perhaps it could be attributed to Jesus himself—to a request or command he made that Peter should deny knowing him, not to deny his divinity but to deny knowing him as the religious rebel the Jewish leaders saw him to be. Why? To ensure Peter's safety as chief apostle and to ensure the continuity and safety of the Quorum of the Twelve.

Some may object that God would never command any of his children to do such a thing, but we do not know all that God knows, nor do we know all that went on in this situation. Moreover, we find interesting contradictions, or seeming contradictions, in other scriptural passages that put this episode in a different light. For example, God commanded Abraham that his wife, Sarah, should tell the Egyptians that she was Abraham's sister so that he would be protected, just as Jesus wanted the apostles protected (Abraham 2:23–25). We also remember Deity commanding Nephi to slay Laban in order to keep a whole nation safe spiritually and to bring forth God's righteous purposes (1 Nephi 4:13). The Prophet Joseph Smith taught:

But we cannot keep all the commandments without

first knowing them, and we cannot expect to know all, or more than we now know unless we comply with or keep those we have already received. That which is wrong under one circumstance, may be, and often is, right under another.

God said, "Thou shalt not kill;" at another time He said, "Thou shalt utterly destroy." This is the principle on which the government of heaven is conducted—by revelation adapted to the circumstances in which the children of the kingdom are placed. Whatever God requires is right, no matter what it is, although we may not see the reason thereof till long after the events transpire. If we seek first the kingdom of God, all good things will be added. So with Solomon: first he asked wisdom, and God gave it him, and with it every desire of his heart, even things which might be considered abominable to all who understand the order of heaven only in part, but which in reality were right because God gave and sanctioned by special revelation. (*Teachings of the Prophet Joseph Smith*, 256)

Remember, by the time of his arrest, Jesus was protective of his apostles, and the safety of the Quorum had become a major concern for him. As we have indicated, in his great high priestly prayer, the Savior prayed for the safety of the apostles. "I pray not that thou shouldest take them out of the world, but that thou shouldest keep them from the evil" (John 17:15). When he was arrested in the garden, he said to the mob, "I have told you that I am he: if therefore ye seek me, let these go their way" (John 18:8). Jesus did not want anything to happen to those who were ordained to take over the earthly leadership of the

Church. He had already averted wholesale slaughter in Gethsemane when first, in the upper room, he restricted to two the number of swords carried by the apostles (Luke 22:38). Later, while being arrested, he told Peter to put away his sword, "for all they that take the sword shall perish with the sword" (Matthew 26:52). It will be remembered that some of the apostles asked, "Lord, shall we smite with the sword?" (Luke 22:49) while Peter went ahead and lopped off Malchus's ear without waiting for an answer.

Jesus had told Peter at the Last Supper that He had prayed that Peter's faith would not fail—and it did not. As President Kimball stated: "Peter was under fire; all the hosts of hell were against him. The die had been cast for the Savior's crucifixion. If Satan could destroy Simon now, what a victory he would score. *Here was the greatest of all living men.* Lucifer wanted to confuse him, frustrate him, limit his prestige, and totally destroy him. However, this was not to be, for he was chosen and ordained to a high purpose in heaven, as was Abraham" (*Peter, My Brother,* 488–89; emphasis added).

Matthew tells us that Peter went to the high priest's palace "to see the end" (Matthew 26:58). The implication is that Peter went as a witness of the last events associated with the life of the mortal Messiah. Had Peter been inclined to cowardice, it seems likely he would not have gone to the palace and put himself in harm's way. How grateful we are to have had Peter there as an eyewitness of that part of the atoning sacrifice.

In sum, it is apparent that Jesus knew of Peter's fearlessness in defending him. He had seen several manifestations of Peter's unswerving, almost reckless, commitment to prevent any physical harm to the Savior. And this was something Jesus knew could get Peter into trouble if it were not tempered. It would put the chief apostle in grave physical danger. Therefore, it is possible that when Jesus told Peter he would deny him thrice before the cock crowed twice, it was not a prediction—it was a command. This is, in fact, a possible reading of the Synoptic texts, according to the grammatical rules of Koine Greek, which is the language in which early manuscripts of the New Testament were written. In their accounts of this episode, Matthew (26:34, 75), Mark (14:30, 72), and Luke (22:34, 61) all use the same verb and verb form, *aparnēse*, which can be read either as an indicative future tense or as an imperative (command) tense. One Latter-day Saint scholar of classical languages arrived at the following conclusion:

> When the Lord had informed the eleven who remained with Him to finish the Last Supper that they would soon be scattered, Peter protested that he would never abandon the Savior, but sooner go to his death. Tradition portrays Christ as then prophesying of the three-time denial of Peter to come that very night (Matthew 26:31–35; Mark 14:27–31; Luke 22:31–34; John 13:36–38). However, close examination of the original Greek of John's account (John 13:38) reveals that the phrase "till thou hast denied me thrice" is structured around the verb ἀρνήσῃ [arnēse], a second person singular future indicative verb form. Virtually the same verb ἀπαρνήσῃ [aparnēse], in the same second person singular future indicative form, appears in Matthew (26:34), Mark (14:30), and Luke (22:34). Although the tense is future, and may accurately be construed as indicating a prediction or prophecy of Peter's future behavior, it is possible that such a rendering is not at all the

meaning of Christ's statement. In Greek, a future tense verb in the second person can also be construed to express a command, just as if it were an imperative form of the verb. This usage is given the grammatical term of the "jussive future." It occurs not infrequently in both classical and *koine* Greek. Accordingly, if the future in these passages is interpreted as a jussive future, then Christ would seem actually to be giving Peter a command to deny knowing Him, and Peter's protestation would seem to reflect his dissatisfaction about such an instruction. This rendering appears very much in keeping with Peter's natural courage. Restraint would test Peter's faith so much more, for he was being refused permission to expose himself to the tribulations that Christ must undertake alone. . . .

When Christ was taken, instead of acting impulsively, Peter did demonstrate great restraint both in not trying to interfere in the process of Jesus' death and in protecting himself that he might live to fulfill his mission. How he must have wanted to wield his sword and free the Savior! How he must have desired to proclaim Jesus as the Christ to those assembled in the courtyard! Although Peter never denied the divinity of Christ, he must have been in tremendous turmoil not to be able to admit to his friendship with Jesus, and could even have felt as if this practically constituted a denial of his friend. Each time Peter was questioned as to his association with Jesus and compelled to deny it, seemingly contradicting his own pledge of loyalty unto death, what faith was put into the charge Christ had given him for the future! Peter was neither impetuous, nor did he lack faith. Quite the opposite. The man who had fearlessly struck with his sword at Gethsemane, was the same man who evidenced fearless and faithful restraint in the courtyard of the high priest. John's telling of the account shows Peter's faith, not his fear. (Hall, *New Testament Witnesses of Christ*, 65–66)

Some might ask, "Why then did Peter weep bitterly after his denial?" Isn't it possible that those were tears of frustration and bitter sorrow in the realization that he was powerless to change the Lord's fate? He had done what needed to be done, but every impulse inside him was to act differently—to prevent the suffering of the Savior. That must have been a bitter pill for Peter to swallow. He wept tears of frustration precisely because he was obedient and also because he was fully aware that he was going to lose his Master to the inevitability of death. In my view, Peter's denial, far from detracting from his stature, greatly adds to it. How grateful we are to a modern prophet and apostle, Spencer W. Kimball, for helping us to look at events in the New Testament differently with the aid of prophetic interpretation.

All the chief priests and elders of the people took counsel against Jesus to put him to death:

And when they had bound him, they led him away, and delivered him to Pontius Pilate the governor.

Then Judas, which had betrayed him, when he saw that he was condemned, repented himself, and brought again the thirty pieces of silver to the chief priests and elders,

Saying, I have sinned in that I have betrayed the innocent blood. And they said, What is that to us? see thou to that.

And he cast down the pieces of silver in the temple, and departed, and went and hanged himself.

And the chief priests took the silver pieces, and said, It is not lawful for to put them into the treasury, because it is the price of blood.

And they took counsel, and bought with them the potter's field, to bury strangers in.

Wherefore that field was called, The field of blood, unto this day.

Then was fulfilled that which was spoken by Jeremy the prophet, saying, And they took the thirty pieces of silver, the price of him that was valued, whom they of the children of Israel did value;

And gave them for the potter's field.

MATTHEW 27:1–10

CHAPTER 5

Pontius Pilate and Judas Iscariot

aving convinced themselves that Jesus of Nazareth was guilty of blasphemy and sedition ("they *all* condemned him to be guilty of death"; Mark 14:64; emphasis added), the Jewish leaders made ready to deliver him to Pontius Pilate. All of the safeguards put into place in the Mosaic law and rabbinic tradition to ensure that the innocent were not made scapegoats or railroaded into conviction—no one-day trials resulting in capital punishment, no self-incrimination or confession without corroborating witnesses who agreed with each other, no hearing before the Sanhedrin in the house of the high priest—all these elements seem to have been deliberately ignored in the case of Jesus.

IRONIES AND CONTRADICTIONS

The ironies—indeed, the contradictions—of Jesus' separate arraignments before Annas and Caiaphas are stunning. Though he was convicted as a result of the testimony of false witnesses, Jesus Christ was and is the "*faithful* witness" (Revelation 1:5; emphasis added). Though the Sanhedrin spoke blasphemously to him, Jesus was truly God. Though he rightly spoke as God, he was convicted of blasphemy against God (Mark 14:62–63). Though he stood before Annas and Caiaphas, who held the title of high priest, Jesus is the true High Priest, the "High Priest of our profession" (Hebrews 3:1).

Everything those false high priests were not, Jesus Christ is—"an high priest . . . who is holy, harmless, undefiled, separate from sinners, and made higher than the heavens" (Hebrews 7:26). Though he was forced to stand before two high priests who considered themselves to be important because they supervised the daily sacrifices in the Temple and entered the Holy of Holies once a year on the Day of Atonement, Jesus himself was the very author of the sacrificial system as well as the great and last sacrifice under the Mosaic law, the fulfillment of the whole system of sacrifice (Alma 34:13–14). The book of Hebrews explains the ways in which Jesus fulfilled the role of the Israelite high priest as well as the system of animal sacrifice, which was a pattern of Jesus' sacrifice:

> Who needeth not daily, as those high priests, to offer up sacrifice, first for his own sins, and then for the people's: for this he did once, when he offered up himself.
>
> It was therefore necessary that the patterns of things in the heavens should be purified with these; but the heavenly things themselves with better sacrifices than these.
>
> For Christ is not entered into the holy places made with hands, which are the figures of the true; but into heaven itself, now to appear in the presence of God for us:

Nor yet that he should offer himself often, as the high priest entereth into the holy place every year with blood of others;

For then must he often have suffered since the foundation of the world: but now once in the end of the world hath he appeared to put away sin by the sacrifice of himself. (Hebrews 7:27; 9:23–26)

Many more ironies and contradictions would be added to the list of the Savior's tribulations in Jerusalem on the eve of Passover. But enough have been discussed already to allow a deeper appreciation of the Prophet Joseph Smith's statement that Jesus Christ "descended in suffering below that which man can suffer; or, in other words, suffered greater sufferings, and was exposed to *more powerful contradictions* than any man can be. But, notwithstanding all this, he kept the law of God, and remained without sin, showing thereby that it is in the power of man to keep the law and remain also without sin" (*Lectures on Faith*, 5:2; emphasis added). If ever a statement applied to Jesus' arraignments in front of Jewish leaders, this one does.

PONTIUS PILATE

With poignant brevity Matthew reports what happened to Jesus after he endured the long night of suffering, accusation, and abuse, which culminated in his being condemned to death by Caiaphas and the council of unrelenting Jewish leaders. "When the morning was come, all the chief priests and elders of the people took counsel against Jesus to put him to death: And when they had bound him, they led him away, and delivered him to Pontius Pilate the governor" (Matthew 27:1–2).

Jesus had prophesied his arraignments in front of Pilate as well as the Jewish council several days before that fateful Friday. As he made his way to Jerusalem for the last time, Jesus warned the Twelve that "the Son of man shall be delivered unto the chief priests, and unto the scribes; and they shall condemn him to death, and *shall deliver him to the Gentiles*" (Mark 10:33; emphasis added). The Savior knew full well what lay ahead before he ever made his triumphal entry into Jerusalem and before he was brought to stand in front of Pilate, one of the Gentiles of whom he spoke.

Pontius Pilate was the Roman governor of Judea from A.D. 26 to 36. Technically, his title was *Praefectus Iudaeae*, "prefect of Judea," according to an inscription found at Caesarea Maritima on the Mediterranean coast. The Passion (from Latin, *passus*, "to suffer") narratives in the Gospels portray him as something of a well-meaning but weak ruler who attempted to shift responsibility for the execution of Jesus from himself to others.

The truth is, Pilate was extremely powerful when he began his rule; he was also cruel and arrogant. When the Roman emperor appointed a governor over an imperial province such as Judea, he invested the appointee with full authority to administer the territory economically, politically, and militarily. In judging Jesus, Pilate was free to decide His guilt or innocence, to adopt or reject the Sanhedrin's decision, or to consult with anyone he wished. The problem was that Pilate had so inflamed his Jewish subjects that he had used up all the goodwill, respect, and political capital he needed to set Jesus free. Ultimately, he chose political expediency. He chose to wash his hands of the situation and not to take the stand he could have taken to free Jesus. He chose not to act on his knowledge and impressions of the Savior's innocence. Ironically, he chose not to oppose the Jewish opinion makers in this instance, although he had done so plenty of other times.

Nonbiblical sources describe Pilate's problems with the Jews, characterizing him as insensitive, offensive, corrupt, irrational, and cruel. Josephus reports that Pilate deeply offended the people and violated Mosaic law when he attached graven images of the emperor to Roman standards within Jerusalem's sacred precincts. He incited a deadly riot when he appropriated funds from the Temple treasury to finance an aqueduct that brought water into the Temple, even though it was needed. According to Philo, the Jewish philosopher-theologian, Pilate incensed the Jews when he installed shields bearing the emperor's name in Herod's former palace in Jerusalem. He was recalled to Rome in A.D. 36 after a massacre of the Samaritans and never again appointed to an important government post.

SUICIDE OF JUDAS

Before describing the Savior's arraignment in front of Pilate, Matthew inserts a unique note regarding the fate of Jesus' betrayer. When Judas saw that Jesus had been condemned by the Jewish council and was being transferred to the Roman governor to secure capital conviction, the gravity of the situation caused a change of heart. He tried to reverse his betrayal and return the paltry sum of thirty pieces of silver, the price of a slave. To his co-conspirators, the chief priests, he confessed his self-realized grievous sin of betraying innocent blood. But they would have none of it—a witness of the truth from the Savior's very betrayer was turned away. Justice and truth were ignored. Distraught, Judas cast the money into the Temple and went out and hanged himself (Matthew 27:3–5).

At some point the chief priests, ever observant of the smallest legal issues when it served their purposes, decided it was not lawful to deposit Judas's blood money in the Temple treasury (never mind that it had originated with them). So, magnanimously, they purchased the potter's field as a cemetery for strangers and in so doing fulfilled another Old Testament prophecy, which Matthew attributed to Jeremiah but which can now be found only in Zechariah: "And I said unto them, If ye think good, give me my price; and if not, forbear. So they weighed for my price thirty pieces of silver. And the Lord said unto me, Cast it unto the potter: a goodly price that I was prised at of them. And I took the thirty pieces of silver, and cast them to the potter in the house of the Lord" (Zechariah 11:12–13).

No definite explanation can be found about why Matthew attributes this prophecy to Jeremiah. Perhaps it was once found in Jeremiah's writings, or perhaps an oral tradition once ascribed its origin to Jeremiah. Whatever its source, however, its impressive fulfillment cannot be denied.

Some scholars have pitted Matthew's version of Judas's death against the apostle Peter's version, which states that Judas, "falling headlong, he burst asunder in the midst, and all his bowels gushed out" (Acts 1:18). The Joseph Smith Translation of Matthew 27:6 indicates that both occurred: "And he . . . went, and hanged himself on a tree. And straightway he fell down, and his bowels gushed out, and he died."

Great questions remain about Judas's motives for betraying the Savior. Various theories favorable to Judas have been proffered about why he betrayed his Master. Perhaps, they say, Judas was attempting to get Jesus to display his messianic powers and authority to hasten the overthrow of the Romans, and so forth. In other words, these theories suggest, Judas was not wicked; he just misunderstood the kind of Messiah Jesus was. It must be remembered, however, that the Gospels of both Luke and John refer to Satan entering "into" Judas—not just influencing him (Luke 22:3; John 13:27). And the Prophet Joseph Smith taught that "the devil has no power over us only as we permit him. The moment we revolt at anything which comes from God, the devil takes power" (*Teachings of the Prophet Joseph Smith*, 181). Certainly, the devil took control of Judas's life at some point.

Similarly, questions remain concerning Judas's ultimate situation in eternity. Some students of the New Testament adhere strictly to the text of the Savior's high priestly prayer as they argue that Judas was guilty of the unpardonable sin. In that prayer Jesus refers to having lost none of those whom the Father had given to him, except "the son of perdition" (John 17:12). It is true that Judas is not liked very much in the Gospels—especially in John (see, for example, John 12:6, in which Judas is referred to as a "thief"). Nonetheless, modern prophets, who possess extraordinary doctrinal acumen, have been cautious in their assessments. President Joseph F. Smith observed:

> Now, if Judas really had known God's power, and had partaken thereof, and did actually "deny the truth" and "defy" that power, "having denied the Holy Spirit after he had received it," and also "denied the Only Begotten," after God had "revealed him" unto him, then there can be no doubt that he "will die the second death."
>
> That Judas did partake of all this knowledge—that

these great truths had been revealed to him—that he had received the Holy Spirit by the gift of God, and was therefore qualified to commit the unpardonable sin, is not at all clear to me. To my mind it strongly appears that not one of the disciples possessed sufficient light, knowledge nor wisdom, at the time of the crucifixion, for either exaltation or condemnation; for it was afterward that their minds were opened to understand the scriptures, and that they were endowed with power from on high; without which they were only children in knowledge, in comparison to what they afterwards become under the influence of the Spirit. (*Gospel Doctrine*, 433)

In harmony with the teachings of President Joseph F. Smith, Elder Bruce R. McConkie wrote: "Only Judas has been lost; and even he, though a son or follower of Satan . . . is probably not a son of perdition in the sense of eternal damnation" (*Mortal Messiah*, 4:112–13).

Whatever Judas's ultimate destiny, we learn important lessons from his situation about the need for constant vigilance against Satan's attempts to influence us and drive a wedge between us and our Master. Judas was a member of the Quorum of the Twelve Apostles, worthy to hold that honored position when he was first chosen by the Savior. But something happened along the way to allow the devil to take control of his life. Constant vigilance against Satan's influence is the price we must pay for spiritual power. The life of Judas teaches us that no one is exempt, not even a member of the Quorum of the Twelve. We also learn from the example of Judas that great personal sorrow inevitably follows wicked actions—sometimes leading to a compounding of personal tragedy (in Judas's case, suicide). As with Judas's, our own actions hardly ever affect just ourselves. Often they affect other people, sometimes even great numbers of others.

One last lesson we learn from Judas's actions is that we may not always be able to explain why once-worthy, faithful, and trusted associates end up doing deceitful, despicable things. President Harold B. Lee taught that

> some of the greatest of our enemies are those within our own ranks. It was the lament of the Master, as he witnessed one of those chosen men, who under inspiration he chose as one of the Twelve, betray him with a kiss. . . . And Jesus could only explain that of the Twelve, meaning Judas, he had a devil.
>
> When we see some of our own today doing similar things, some who have been recognized and honored in the past as teachers and leaders who later fall by the wayside, our hearts are made sore and tender. But sometimes we have to say just like the Master said, "The devil must have entered into them." (Conference Report, October 1973, 166)

And the whole multitude of them arose, and led him unto Pilate.

And they began to accuse him, saying, We found this fellow perverting the nation, and forbidding to give tribute to Caesar, saying that he himself is Christ a King.

And Pilate asked him, saying, Art thou the King of the Jews? And he answered him and said, Thou sayest it.

Then said Pilate to the chief priests and to the people, I find no fault in this man.

And they were the more fierce, saying, He stirreth up the people, teaching throughout all Jewry, beginning from Galilee to this place.

When Pilate heard of Galilee, he asked whether the man were a Galilaean.

And as soon as he knew that he belonged unto Herod's jurisdiction, he sent him to Herod, who himself also was at Jerusalem at that time.

And when Herod saw Jesus, he was exceeding glad: for he was desirous to see him of a long season, because he had heard many things of him; and he hoped to have seen some miracle done by him.

Then he questioned with him in many words; but he answered him nothing.

And the chief priests and scribes stood and vehemently accused him.

And Herod with his men of war set him at nought, and mocked him, and arrayed him in a gorgeous robe, and sent him again to Pilate.

And the same day Pilate and Herod were made friends together: for before they were at enmity between themselves.

LUKE 23:1–12

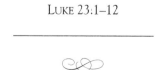

CHAPTER 6

Arraignment before Pilate and Herod

The decision of the Jewish council to take Jesus to Pilate at an early hour on Friday morning bespeaks the urgency with which the chief priests and the Jewish council wanted Jesus disposed of. Perhaps they figured the early hour would also impress Pilate that the situation was extremely dangerous and needed to be acted upon immediately. It was probably well before 6 A.M.—considered the first hour of the day in most eastern Mediterranean cultures—when the contingent arrived with their prisoner. John provides the setting: "Then led they Jesus from Caiaphas unto the hall of judgment: and it was early; and they themselves went not into the judgment hall, lest they should be defiled; but that they might eat the passover. Pilate then went out unto them, and said, What accusation bring ye against this man?" (John 18:28–29).

Because Galilean Jews reckoned their days from sunrise to sunrise, Jesus and the apostles had already eaten their Passover meal Thursday evening. But Jews in Judea counted their days from sundown to sundown and had not yet celebrated their Passover dinner, which they expected to do later that Friday

(MacArthur, *Murder of Jesus*, 163). Therefore, as John points out, the members of the council taking Jesus to Pilate felt they could not, according to rabbinic law, enter a Gentile residence without becoming ceremonially unclean and therefore unable to eat the Passover meal. Thus, they met Pilate outside his Jerusalem residence.

There is some debate over the location of Pilate's judgment hall. Roman prefects usually lived in Caesarea Maritima, west of Jerusalem, on the Mediterranean coast (Acts 23:35) and also had an official residence, or praetorium, in Jerusalem. Two buildings, both built by Herod the Great (died 4 B.C.), are candidates for having been Pilate's judgment hall. Some scholars argue vigorously for the Antonia Fortress. It was like a palace, according to Josephus, and occupied the northwest corner of the Temple Mount, overlooking the sanctuary and the courtyard of the Temple. Literary evidence, on the other hand, points to the other building, Herod's Palace, as the place where Pilate was living, even though it is not the traditional location. It was newer and more opulent than the Antonia Fortress and situated on the western side of the walled city, in what is now the Armenian Quarter of the Old City. Philo, in one of his writings, tells us plainly that "on the occasion of a Jewish feast Pilate was residing in 'Herod's Palace in the Holy City,' which he describes as 'the residence of the prefects'" (Wilkinson, *Jerusalem As Jesus Knew It,* 140). Thus, He who was regarded as the lowliest of prisoners was marched in shackles from the opulent palace of Caiaphas the high priest to the opulent palace of Pilate the Roman prefect, although in reality He was the King of the universe.

The case against Jesus likely proceeded with Pilate standing or sitting on a *bema,* or raised platform, in front of the accused and his accusers. We know that Pilate's final sentence was also delivered from the *bema* (Matthew 27:19), or in other words, from "the judgment seat in a place that is called the Pavement [in Greek, *lithostroton*], but in the Hebrew, Gabbatha" (John 19:13). The two words used here have different meanings: *Lithostroton* is a Greek term meaning "stone pavement"; *Gabbatha* is actually an Aramaic term meaning "raised place." We may therefore assume that "the regular procedure at the Palace was to use a raised outdoor paved area nearby, on which the resident Palace official set up a platform for his public appearances. This guess is made considerably more probable by our knowledge that Josephus tells us of two prefects who addressed angry crowds in Jerusalem from a platform: Pilate in about A.D. 30 and Florus in A.D. 66" (Wilkinson, *Jerusalem as Jesus Knew It*, 141).

Pilate undoubtedly knew something of Jesus' difficulties, if for no other reason than Roman soldiers were almost certainly involved in the arrest. But in that early hour on Friday morning when Jesus was standing in front of him, Pilate asked the accompanying Jewish council: "What accusation bring ye against this man?" (John 18:29). Luke implies that the entire council that had been in on the second Jewish arraignment (involving Caiaphas) began to accuse Jesus of sedition, or treason, saying, "We found this fellow perverting the nation, and forbidding to give tribute to Caesar, saying that he himself is Christ a King" (Luke 23:2). Their charge was not truthful, for just a few days earlier Jesus had taught: "Render therefore unto Caesar the things which are Caesar's" (Matthew 22:21). They did not press the charge of blasphemy, although the term *Christ*, or *Messiah*, might have had political or military connotations.

JESUS' INNOCENCE VERSUS
JEWISH VEHEMENCE

The Jewish assembly knew that reference to blasphemy would do nothing to elicit the approval they desired for Jesus' execution. The Romans had many gods, each to be given its due, and they knew nothing of blasphemy in the sense that the Jews meant it. But the Jewish leaders did use circular reasoning to try to force Pilate to agree to their request, saying, "If he were not a malefactor [criminal], we would not have delivered him up unto thee" (John 18:30). The arrogance of their argument is really quite stunning. They were saying, in effect, "Look, the fact that we're bringing him to you should be evidence enough to convict him. Don't ask any questions. Just do what we're telling you!"

Knowing what the Jewish leaders wanted, Pilate told them to take Jesus "and judge him according to your law" (John 18:31). He saw no reason to become embroiled in what he perceived to be an internal dispute among a people he cared little about. As a politician he did not want any part of a situation that could only make him look bad. The response of the Jewish leaders to Pilate's proposal is also significant: "It is not lawful for us to put any man to death" (John 18:31).

This scene is amazing. Here was Pontius Pilate, the most powerful man in Judea, offering the Jewish council a free hand, giving them the opportunity to deal with Jesus on the basis of their own customs and laws. But they were not satisfied. They wanted, even demanded, a Roman execution. Reasons for this arc probably complex, but among the most important is surely the Jewish leaders' desire for a shield to hide behind. They feared the people and feared public opinion about Jesus (Matthew 26:5). If Pilate acceded to their wishes, they could attribute the death of Jesus to Roman decisions and Roman action. Also, if the Jews were to put Jesus to death, they would stone him, but the Romans would crucify him. Therefore, if the Romans could be made to take responsibility for the execution of Jesus within the Jewish leaders' self-imposed time constraints, they could avoid violating the Jewish regulations that would declare them ritually defiled because they had stoned someone just before the celebration of Passover. Whatever the Jews' reasons for wanting the Romans to execute Jesus, one more thing is certain. Their demands guaranteed the crucifixion of the Savior and fulfilled his own prophecy "which he spake, signifying what death he should die" (John 18:32).

Jesus' ultimate fate was no surprise to himself or to God the Father. Both Jesus and his Father knew that he would die by crucifixion. That had been prophesied by seers long before Jesus was born. Around 600 B.C. Nephi declared that he saw the Messiah "lifted up upon the cross and slain for the sins of the world" (1 Nephi 11:33). And King Benjamin testified: "And he shall be called Jesus Christ, the Son of God, the Father of heaven and earth, the Creator of all things from the beginning; and his mother shall be called Mary. And lo, he cometh unto his own, that salvation might come unto the children of men even through faith on his name; and even after all this they shall consider him a man, and say that he hath a devil, and shall scourge him, and shall crucify him" (Mosiah 3:8–9). Even more significantly, during the first year of his public ministry, Jesus himself said that the already ancient episode of Moses raising the brass serpent in the wilderness was a symbol of his forthcoming crucifixion: "And as Moses lifted up the serpent in the wilderness, even so must the Son of man be lifted up" (John 3:14).

Thus, Jesus walked in the shadow of the cross his whole life, knowing ahead of time how he would die. As Elder Neal A. Maxwell reminds us, prophecy "springs from very exact knowledge in the mind of the Lord Jesus Christ and God the Eternal Father, and it is surely very exacting in our lives as we experience its fulfillment" (*All These Things Shall Give Thee Experience*, 22). It was certainly proving to be very exacting for the Savior.

As with the Savior, so with us. There are no surprises to God when it comes to our lives. He knows all things that shall befall us, from the beginning to the end (Helaman 8:8). He knows where and when and under what circumstances each one of his spirit sons and daughters will be born and under what conditions each will live (Acts 17:26). He knows how and when we will die. He knows all things because all things are present before his eyes (D&C 38:2).

And because God knows all things, has all power, wisdom, and understanding (Alma 26:35), we may exercise unbounded confidence in him, in his love for us, and in his power to bring to pass all that is in our best interests. The Prophet Joseph Smith taught:

> Without the knowledge of all things God would not be able to save any portion of his creatures; for it is by reason of the knowledge which he has of all things, from the beginning to the end, that enables him to give that understanding to his creatures by which they are made partakers of eternal life; and if it were not for the idea existing in the minds of men that God had all knowledge it would be impossible for them to exercise faith in him.
>
> And it is not less necessary that men should have the idea of the existence of the attribute power in the Deity; for unless God had power over all things, and was

able by his power to control all things, and thereby deliver his creatures who put their trust in him from the power of all beings that might seek their destruction, whether in heaven, on earth, or in hell, men could not be saved. But with the idea of the existence of this attribute planted in the mind, men feel as though they had nothing to fear who put their trust in God, believing that he has power to save all who come to him to the very uttermost. . . .

For inasmuch as God possesses the attribute knowledge, he can make all things known to his saints necessary for their salvation; and as he possesses the attribute power, he is able thereby to deliver them from the power of all enemies; and seeing, also, that justice is an attribute of the Deity, he will deal with them upon the principles of righteousness and equity, and a just reward will be granted unto them for all their afflictions and sufferings for truth's sake. (*Lectures on Faith*, 4:11–12, 17)

Coupled with God's knowledge and power is his overriding attribute of love. God is love, as we have been told starkly (1 John 4:8, 16). I take this to mean that God is so full of love, so infused with this radiating quality, that all of God's other attributes and characteristics are shaped by, influenced by, and mediated through his love. Again, from the *Lectures on Faith*:

And lastly, but not less important to the exercise of faith in God, is the idea that he is love; for with all the other excellencies in his character, without this one to influence them, they could not have such powerful dominion over the minds of men; but when the idea is planted in the mind that he is love, who cannot see the just ground that men of every nation, kindred, and tongue, have to exercise faith in God so as to obtain to eternal life? (3:24)

Because we know that all God thinks and does is influenced by his perfect love, we may also rest assured that the horror of Christ's crucifixion, and the still greater horror of Christ's knowing beforehand that he was facing the surety of crucifixion, was necessary. It was part of our Heavenly Father's plan from the beginning and was foreordained to be of supreme benefit to us. "He doeth not anything save it be for the benefit of the world; for he loveth the world, even that he layeth down his own life that he may draw all men unto him. Wherefore, he commandeth none that they shall not partake of his salvation" (2 Nephi 26:24).

CAPITAL PUNISHMENT

How much authority the Sanhedrin possessed to carry out capital punishment has been much debated. New Testament passages, especially Acts 21 and 22, as well as certain passages in Josephus support John's statement that Jewish councils in first-century Palestine did not possess decision-making authority in capital cases. The three most significant exceptions suggesting Jewish authorities did have some authority in such cases are the stoning of Stephen (Acts 6–7), the stoning of Paul (Acts 14:19), and the well-documented evidence (both archaeological and literary) of signs in Greek and Latin on the balustrade, or walled barrier, surrounding the Temple sanctuary forbidding all Gentiles, on penalty of death, to go into restricted holy areas beyond the Court of the Gentiles in the Temple Mount courtyard.

These three exceptions might be explained on the basis of two circumstances, however. First, the Romans granted standing approval of capital punishment for certain narrowly defined and undisputed offenses committed in public view (such as Gentiles bringing upon themselves their own death by ignoring warnings of restricted areas on the Temple Mount). Second, Jewish councils or groups of people motivated by religious zeal occasionally overstepped their authority. According to well-known New Testament scholar F. F. Bruce, "the right of jurisdiction in capital cases was most jealously reserved by provincial governors; permission to provincials to exercise it was a very rare concession, conceded only to such privileged communities as free cities within the empire. Jerusalem was no free city, and a turbulent province like Judaea was most unlikely to be granted such a concession" (*New Testament History*, 200). Thus, Stephen's later execution was a mob action precisely because the Romans did reserve the right to administer capital punishment and the mob did not want to wait for Roman legal machinery to do its work.

Whatever actual powers over life and death were invested in Jewish leaders during the years Jesus of Nazareth inhabited Roman Palestine, one thing is certain: Caiaphas and his council tried to force the Roman governor to implement the death penalty by charging Jesus with sedition.

Jesus' Dialogue with Pilate

On this Friday morning, Pilate saw through the ruse. He saw that Jesus was not a threat to Rome, after spending only a few minutes alone with the Savior. He entered the Praetorium with Jesus, leaving the Jewish assembly outside, and began with a significant question: "Art thou the King of the Jews?" (John 18:33). The exchange that followed is reported by John:

Jesus answered him, Sayest thou this thing of thyself, or did others tell it thee of me?

Pilate answered, Am I a Jew? Thine own nation and the chief priests have delivered thee unto me: what hast thou done?

Jesus answered, My kingdom is not of this world: if my kingdom were of this world, then would my servants fight, that I should not be delivered to the Jews: but now is my kingdom not from hence.

Pilate therefore said unto him, Art thou a king then? Jesus answered, Thou sayest that I am a king. To this end was I born, and for this cause came I into the world, that I should bear witness unto the truth. Every one that is of the truth heareth my voice.

Pilate saith unto him, What is truth? And when he had said this, he went out again unto the Jews, and saith unto them, I find in him no fault at all. (John 18:34–38)

In the presence of his Roman inquisitor, Jesus bore down in pure testimony regarding His divine identity and mission. Indeed, he was King of the Jews. "To this end was I born," he declared (John 18:37), which was absolutely true. "At the time of the Savior's birth, Israel was ruled by alien monarchs. The rights of the royal Davidic family were unrecognized; and the ruler of the Jews was an appointee of Rome. Had Judah been a free and independent nation, ruled by her rightful sovereign, Joseph the carpenter would have been her crowned king; and his lawful successor to the throne would have been Jesus of Nazareth, the King of the Jews" (Talmage, *Jesus the Christ*, 87). But Jesus also declared to Pilate that His real kingdom was "not of this world" (John 18:36); it was not the Roman Empire. He further indicated that his whole-souled effort centered on bearing "witness unto the truth"—meaning religious truth, or the eternal verities, of his Father's plan of redemption.

This answer must have struck a nerve with Pilate, and he likely got the philosophical import of Jesus' statement, for he responded, "What is truth?" (John 18:38). With so many religious systems in the Roman Empire and so many gods being worshiped, it is not hard to imagine Pilate asking his question in a tone of sarcastic musing. Still, Jesus evinced nothing treasonous in either his discourse or demeanor.

Surely, Pilate had to wonder why Jesus posed such a threat. To execute him as an insurrectionist would be absurd. And surely the force of Jesus' personality alone was persuasive evidence of his greatness and uniqueness. Pilate returned outside to the open-air judgment seat, having received a deposition from the Accused, the likes of which he had never before experienced. How could he not declare Jesus to be innocent?

Pilate faced the Jewish crowd and proclaimed that he found no fault in Jesus whatsoever. The Jewish reaction to Pilate's declaration of the Savior's innocence is what we might expect. They became "more fierce," more intense in their accusations, and more adamant that Jesus was a huge threat to the peace of the entire country and beyond. "He stirreth up the people," they cried, "teaching throughout all Jewry, beginning from Galilee to this place" (Luke 23:5).

THE FELLOWSHIP OF HIS SILENCE

Noteworthy again is the vehemence of Jesus' accusers, principally the chief priests, as they continued to press for his execution. No less significant is the Savior's silence. "And the chief priests accused him of many things: but he answered nothing.

81

And Pilate asked him again, saying, Answerest thou nothing? behold how many things they witness against thee. But Jesus yet answered nothing; so that Pilate marvelled" (Mark 15:3–5).

The image here is stark and heart-wrenching: Jesus suffering in silence, alone, without defenders, without help. Once again Isaiah's prophecy was fulfilled: "He was oppressed, and he was afflicted, yet he opened not his mouth: he is brought as a lamb to the slaughter, and as a sheep before her shearers is dumb, so he openeth not his mouth" (Isaiah 53:7).

Even Pilate was "surprised at the submissive yet majestic demeanor of Jesus" (Talmage, *Jesus the Christ*, 633). Modern disciples also marvel at Jesus' meekness. He took what was dished out. He exercised poise in the face of provocation. He suffered silently, knowing, as many in our day know, that sometimes silence can be the only response to trials, tribulations, and hardships. Others will not, cannot, understand. Some will not care. A few might even be inclined to think we had brought on the misery ourselves. But there is One with whom we have fellowship, One who knows silent suffering, One who hurts when we hurt, because he experienced the hurt before we did. Perhaps, it is in these moments of silent suffering and submissive meekness that we come to know God best, the time when He tutors us the most. After all, did not he who knows all things make the link between silence and the knowledge of his existence and power—in two separate dispensations, in fact? "Be still, and know that I am God," he declared (Psalm 46:10; D&C 101:16). If we try as hard as we can to endure our trials well, reviling not when we are reviled, assailing not when we are assailed, rendering not evil for evil or railing for railing, suffering silently without murmuring, whining, or feeling sorry for ourselves, then God will exalt us on high (1 Peter 2:23; 3:9; D&C 121:8).

Peter, the chief apostle, who knew something about silent suffering, taught that the trial of our faith was "much more precious than of gold that perisheth, though it be tried with fire" (1 Peter 1:7). He knew we must become like the Savior and endure our trials patiently. "For this is thankworthy, if a man for conscience toward God endure grief, suffering wrongfully. For what glory is it, if, when ye be buffeted for your faults, ye shall take it patiently? but if, when ye do well, and suffer for it, ye take it patiently, this is acceptable with God" (1 Peter 2:19–20). Finally, Peter taught that once we have entered the Savior's fellowship of suffering, we must love and serve one another, helping one another through our trials (1 Peter 1:22).

No less significant than our silence in suffering is our silence in spiritual experiences. We have been counseled not to talk much about sacred things or private spiritual experiences. President Howard W. Hunter, a man well acquainted with both personal suffering and powerful spiritual experiences, counseled: "I have watched a great many of my brethren over the years and we have shared some rare and unspeakable spiritual experiences together. Those experiences have all been different, each special in its own way, and such sacred moments may or may not be accompanied by tears. Very often they are, but sometimes they are accompanied by *total silence*" ("Eternal Investments"; emphasis added).

Silent appreciation is often the most appropriate, most Christlike response to transcendent spiritual experiences, just as silence is often the best response to private trials—be they physical or spiritual. We are never more like the Savior when we override the impulse to tell others either what profound personal experiences we enjoy or to complain about what great trials we are enduring. The Lord's age-old counsel is still timely when it comes to responding to both supernal spiritual experiences and profoundly wrenching trials: "Be still, and know that I am God" (Psalm 46:10).

JESUS BEFORE HEROD

Pilate came close to helping the Savior by defending him to his accusers. But in the end, Pilate chose a way out. Personal preservation took precedence over principle. He sought to transfer responsibility to someone else—he sought a scapegoat. "When Pilate heard of Galilee, he asked whether the man were a Galilaean. And as soon as he knew that he belonged unto Herod's jurisdiction, he sent him to Herod, who himself also was at Jerusalem at that time" (Luke 23:6–7). And so Jesus was shunted off in shackles to Herod Antipas, son of Herod the Great, tetrarch of Galilee and Perea, who was in town for the feast of the Passover. Though perhaps not as blood-thirsty a man as his father, Antipas was despicable in his own right.

Though Pilate did not like Herod Antipas, it is easy to see how political circumstances would have dictated to Pilate the prudence of involving Herod at this point. The case of the Jewish leaders versus Jesus of Nazareth was a potential political fiasco, or worse, for Pontius Pilate. He could not simply dismiss it for fear of provoking the Jews again and lending credibility to mounting doubts about his ability and fitness to rule Judea. Philo tells how Pilate "feared lest [the Jewish leaders] might in reality go on an embassy to the emperor, and might impeach him with respect to other particulars of his government, in respect of his corruption, and his acts of insolence, and his rapine, and his habit of insulting people, and his cruelty, and his continual murders of people untried and uncondemned, and his never-ending and gratuitous, and most grievous inhumanity" (*Legatio ad Gaium*, 302).

Pilate had already provoked his subjects as well as Rome over several offenses that demonstrated his insensitivity and poor judgment. He was known to be ruthless and cruel. Luke mentions an incident involving "Galilaeans, whose blood Pilate mingled with their sacrifices" (Luke 13:1), indicating perhaps that the governor had some Jews from Jesus' home region killed on the Temple Mount as they participated in one of the feasts. We know nothing else about this, except that Galilee was a noted hotbed of insurrectionists, zealots, and terrorist activity against Rome, and perhaps Pilate took extraordinary measures over some threat, perceived or real.

Perhaps the sternest rebuke Pilate had received from the emperor in Rome, Tiberius Caesar, came as a result of the "gold shields" incident. Pilate had some gilded shields made, dedicated them to Tiberius, and hung them in Herod's palace where Pilate stayed in Jerusalem. The inscription on the shields contained the traditional titles of the emperor, one of which attributed to him divine standing, or godhood. This was so offensive to Pilate's monotheistic subjects that they threatened to protest directly to the emperor. Outraged (and worried), Pilate wrote preemptively to Tiberius, putting the best possible spin he could on the volatile situation. Confirming Pilate's worst fears, Tiberius wrote a scathing letter back, as Philo reported: "Immediately, without putting any thing off till the next day, [Tiberius] wrote a letter reproaching and reviling [Pilate] in the most bitter manner for his act of unprecedented audacity and wickedness, and commanding him immediately to take down the shields and to convey them away from the metropolis of Judaea to Caesarea" (*Legatio ad Gaium*, 305). The Jewish leaders knew they could use Pilate's increasingly tenuous position with the emperor as leverage in pressing their charges against Jesus.

It is no surprise, therefore, that Pilate thought of a way to extricate himself from the ticklish business that had real potential to bring down his government. Jesus was from Galilee. Technically, Galilee lay outside Pilate's jurisdiction. If he sent Jesus to Herod, the tetrarch of Galilee, he might be able to dump the problem in Herod's lap. Not only that, but if Pilate sent Jesus to Herod, who wanted to meet the Savior (in hopes of witnessing a miracle), and Pilate could make it look as if he were showing a courtesy to the tetrarch, he might be able to mend a poor relationship that existed between them, the Roman governor and the Jewish ruler.

> And when Herod saw Jesus, he was exceeding glad: for he was desirous to see him of a long season, because he had heard many things of him; and he hoped to have seen some miracle done by him.
>
> Then he questioned with him in many words; but he answered him nothing.
>
> And the chief priests and scribes stood and vehemently accused him.
>
> And Herod with his men of war set him at nought, and mocked him, and arrayed him in a gorgeous robe, and sent him again to Pilate.
>
> And the same day Pilate and Herod were made friends together: for before they were at enmity between themselves. (Luke 23:8–12)

The vehemence of the chief priests and scribes again occupies center stage. Jesus had already stood in silent refutation of their accusations. Now he stood in silent rebuke of the tetrarch of Galilee and Perea. I believe, along with Elder James E. Talmage, that Jesus not only disliked Herod but felt utter contempt for him. He had murdered Jesus' cousin, John the Baptist, and had tried to kill Jesus himself. He deserved no response or respect from the Son of God, whose silence distinguished Herod in the annals of history, as Elder Talmage notes:

> The chief priests and scribes vehemently voiced their accusations; but not a word was uttered by the Lord. Herod is the only character in history to whom Jesus is known to have applied a personal epithet of contempt. "Go ye and tell that fox," He once said to certain Pharisees who had come to Him with the story that Herod intended to kill him. As far as we know, Herod is further distinguished as the only being who saw Christ face to face and spoke to Him, yet never heard His voice. For penitent sinners, weeping women, prattling children, for the scribes, the Pharisees, the Sadducees, the rabbis, for the perjured high priest and his obsequious and insolent underling, and for Pilate the pagan, Christ had words—of comfort or instruction, of warning or rebuke, of protest or denunciation—yet for Herod the fox He had but disdainful and kingly silence. (*Jesus the Christ*, 636)

When Herod could see that he would get nothing out of Jesus, he and his "men-at-arms" ridiculed and mocked the Savior, sarcastically dressed him in an elegant robe, sent him back to Pilate, having "found nothing in Jesus to warrant condemnation" (Talmage, *Jesus the Christ*, 636)—and, more ironic yet, Herod became friends with Pilate over the incident.

Pilate's attempt to rid himself of Jesus' case gracefully had failed. He would have to deal squarely with the God of the universe. It was, in its own way, a burden no other ruler has ever had to face.

Pilate said unto them, Whom will ye that I release unto you? Barabbas, or Jesus which is called Christ?

When he was set down on the judgment seat, his wife sent unto him, saying, Have thou nothing to do with that just man: for I have suffered many things this day in a dream because of him.

But the chief priests and elders persuaded the multitude that they should ask Barabbas, and destroy Jesus.

The governor answered and said unto them, Whether of the twain will ye that I release unto you? They said, Barabbas.

Pilate saith unto them, What shall I do then with Jesus which is called Christ? They all say unto him, Let him be crucified.

When Pilate saw that he could prevail nothing, but that rather a tumult was made, he took water, and washed his hands before the multitude, saying, I am innocent of the blood of this just person: see ye to it.

Then answered all the people, and said, His blood be on us, and on our children.

Then released he Barabbas unto them: and when he had scourged Jesus, he delivered him to be crucified.

Then the soldiers of the governor took Jesus into the common hall, and gathered unto him the whole band of soldiers.

And they stripped him, and put on him a scarlet robe.

And when they had platted a crown of thorns, they put it upon his head, and a reed in his right hand: and they bowed the knee before him, and mocked him, saying, Hail, King of the Jews!

And they spit upon him, and took the reed, and smote him on the head.

MATTHEW 27:17, 19–22, 24–30

CHAPTER 7

The Final Verdict

T he meeting between Herod and Jesus must have been short, since Jesus did not speak. Undoubtedly upset by such condemning silence, Herod had the Savior mocked again, arrayed in a robe that some modern authorities suppose was white, the usual color of dress among Jewish nobility, and sent him back to Pilate—who was now forced to act (Luke 23:11). The robe Herod used was different from the purple one used later by the Roman soldiers to mock Jesus yet again after his second arraignment before Pilate (Matthew 27:27–28). White is a premier symbol of purity and divinity (John 20:12), and though Herod meant its use as a statement of irony, it rightly identified the purest of our Heavenly Father's children.

We can imagine that Pilate was surprised and frustrated when Jesus showed up again so quickly at the Praetorium, perhaps feeling that he had had more than enough of this never-ending situation. Pilate called together the Jewish leaders who constituted Jesus' original accusers as well as others who had by this time joined the ranks of what was fast becoming a mob. He declared to everyone assembled that there were now two independent witnesses—both himself and the people's own Jewish ruler, Herod—attesting the Savior's innocence of any crime worthy of death (Luke 23:13–14). Therefore, he, Pilate, would punish Jesus in Roman fashion—by whipping rather than the much more severe scourging that always preceded crucifixion—and release him in accord with a custom that was invoked at feast time.

RELEASE OF BARABBAS

John's Gospel is clear that the custom of releasing a prisoner at Passover time was a Jewish one (John 18:39). And the Greek text of Mark 15:6 indicates it was "usually" done, meaning the custom was in place long before Jesus' situation had arisen. Pilate seems to have attempted to use the custom at this point as a last-ditch effort to get out from under the tremendous burden of Jesus' trial while saving face at the same time. He was under great pressure not just from the Jewish council but now also from his wife, Procula, whose name we learn from nonbiblical Roman texts. With rapidly increasing intensity, the Jews demanded that Jesus be executed, while Procula anxiously pressed for Pilate to leave Jesus alone! "When he was set down on the judgment seat, his wife sent unto him, saying, Have thou nothing to do with that just man: for I have suffered many things this day in a dream because of him" (Matthew 27:19). Dreams are an important source of personal revelation, and we do not doubt that Pilate's wife received some kind of witness that Jesus was an innocent man and perhaps much more than that. Because she attested to Jesus' innocence through her dream, she was later honored as a saint by the Greek Orthodox Church (*Harper's Bible Dictionary*, s.v. "Pilate, Pontius," 559).

Pilate proposed a brilliant solution. He offered the Jewish assemblage a choice for release: Jesus of Nazareth, who was reputed to be the Messiah (Matthew 27:17), whose guilt was questionable at best, and whose popularity with the common people had been demonstrated a week before during his triumphal entry (Matthew 21:1–11); or Barabbas, an evil and notorious convicted criminal (Matthew 27:16). Surely, the Jewish crowd would choose to release Jesus of Nazareth. But their leaders had been inciting the crowd: "The chief priests and elders persuaded the multitude that they should ask Barabbas, and destroy Jesus. The governor answered and said unto them, Whether of the twain will ye that I release unto you? They said, Barabbas" (Matthew 27:20–21).

The irony of Barabbas's release is so great as to need little explication, but there are ironies beyond the obvious ones:

1. The given name of Barabbas was Yehoshua, or Jesus, the same as the Savior's. An ancient variant reading of the text of Matthew 27:16–17 preserves the full name: "Jesus Barabbas." And the early church theologian Origen (died A.D. 254) implies that the full name appeared in most of the manuscripts of his day. Scholars point out that under these circumstances a much more dramatic reading of Matthew 27:17 was originally intended: "Which Jesus do you want: the son of Abba, or the self-styled Messiah?" (*Anchor Bible Dictionary*, s.v. "Barrabas," 1:607).

2. The term *Barabbas* means, literally, "son of [Aramaic, *bar*] the father [Aramaic, *abba*]." Jesus *was* the true and literal Son of the Father. The angry, stirred-up mob chose to release one Jesus, son of the father, rather than the other Jesus, Son of the Father.

3. Barabbas was guilty of sedition (Luke 23:19, 25) but was

91

freed; Jesus was falsely accused of sedition (Luke 23:2) but was sentenced to death.

4. Barabbas was the fulfillment of the ritual scapegoat of the sacrificial rites performed on the Day of Atonement—the animal led to the wilderness and released; Jesus was the fulfillment of the goat sacrificed on the Temple altar as the sin offering representing the guilt of the people (Leviticus 16:7–22).

5. The Greek word used in Mark 15:13 to denote the cry of the crowd for innocent Jesus' execution in preference to that of the guilty Barabbas is the same word used when the crowd greeted Jesus in messianic tones (Mark 11:9) less than a week before, during his triumphal entry into Jerusalem (Brown, *Death of the Messiah*, 1:824).

Jesus was the embodiment of everything that is good and right and just and pure, while Barabbas seems to have been the embodiment of everything that is not—he was, in fact, the opposite of everything good, right, just, and pure. And yet, the bloodthirsty crowd called for the release of Barabbas. They would have nothing less than the destruction of righteousness in the person of Jesus Christ.

Pilate was now unalterably stuck, and he knew it. Trying one more time to secure the release of Jesus while saving his own neck politically, he spoke to the crowd and uttered the most haunting and important of all questions ever asked, "What shall I do then with Jesus which is called Christ?" (Matthew 27:22). For every modern disciple, is not this the question of the ages—the question of questions? Is it not the question that everyone will someday have to answer? Is it not *the* one question no one will be able to ignore? How will each individual—every man, woman, and child, every saint, sage, and sinner who has ever lived on the earth—choose to regard Jesus of Nazareth? What shall each person do with the name of Jesus Christ? Or, as the Savior himself posed the question, "What think ye of Christ?" (Matthew 22:42).

The response of the Jewish crowd to Pilate's question is as haunting as the question itself. They *all* shouted to Pilate, "Crucify him, crucify him" (Luke 23:21; Matthew 27:22). Pilate's rejoinder to their blood-curdling cries for crucifixion should have given pause to the mob to reconsider their bloodthirsty demands and haunted them long after as well, but apparently it did not. Pilate asked simply: "Why, what evil hath he done?" (Matthew 27:23; Mark 15:14). That the crowd became even more loud and angry can only be attributed to the unrelenting influence of the prince of darkness. "And they cried out the more exceedingly, Crucify him" (Mark 15:14; Matthew 27:23; Luke 23:21). The ugly crowd was about to get its way, the Jewish leaders were about to get their way, and Satan was about to get his way. But his way is unadulterated selfishness, "for he seeketh that all men might be miserable like unto himself" (2 Nephi 2:27). Satan has absolutely no interest in the happiness, peace, or welfare of others. The angry Jewish crowd is witness enough of that.

HAND WASHING: AN ANCIENT CONNECTION

The voices and workings of the chief priests now prevailed without equivocation over the voices of reason and inspiration (Luke 23:23). Under the direction of the chief priests, and undoubtedly at their instigation, the volatile Jewish crowd would have none of Pilate's alternatives or counterproposals. When Pilate could see that he "could prevail nothing" (Matthew 27:24), that he would not succeed, and that he needed to placate the tumultuous crowd to prevent a riot, he gave in to their demands, released Barabbas, scourged Jesus as the official prelude to his crucifixion, and then delivered him up to his sentence of death. But not before Pilate acted out his most famous gesture. He "took water, and washed his hands before the multitude, saying, I am innocent of the blood of this just person: see ye to it. Then answered all the people, and said, His blood be on us, and on our children" (Matthew 27:24–25).

There are several examples in ancient Greek and Roman texts of washing oneself as a symbolic demonstration of absolving oneself of guilt or responsibility for the shedding of another person's blood. Educated Romans, including Pilate, would probably have been familiar with these examples. And the governor may have invoked the procedure because of this ancient practice in the classical world. The symbolism is not difficult to understand. The literal act of washing removed, metaphorically, the fault or responsibility for another person's death. But Pilate may also have had Jewish culture in mind when he performed his ceremonial hand washing, in an effort to make a dramatic impression on Jewish leaders who knew the practice from their study of the Torah. Deuteronomy prescribes ceremonial hand washing by city elders over the carcass of a sacrificed heifer as a sign that their city was not responsible for the death of a slain man: "And all the elders of that city, that are next unto the slain man, shall wash their hands over the heifer that is beheaded in the valley: And they shall answer and say, Our hands have not shed this blood, neither have our eyes seen it. Be merciful, O Lord, unto thy people Israel, whom thou hast redeemed, and lay not innocent blood unto thy people of Israel's charge. And the blood shall be forgiven them" (Deuteronomy 21:6–8).

Whether Pilate could have seen himself in the place of the Israelite city elders and Jesus in the place of the sacrificial heifer seems doubtful; however, Pilate's hand-washing ceremony that

Friday morning in Jerusalem does seem to be a partial fulfillment of the reason the Mosaic prescription was first instituted. From ancient times it had pointed to a specific episode in Christ's life, whether the Israelites knew it or not.

The retort of the multitude after Pilate symbolically absolved himself of responsibility for Jesus' death is chilling indeed. In fact, it is the opposite of the expected response of the people as outlined in Deuteronomy 21:8. Instead of saying, "Be merciful, O Lord, unto thy people Israel, whom thou has redeemed, and lay not innocent blood unto thy people . . . ," the crowd called for the responsibility for the blood of Jesus to be laid upon them and their children! Was this a calculated and purposeful contradiction to the verses in Deuteronomy, which had to have been known to at least some of the Jews in the crowd? Was their answer suggested by the chief priests? We do not know. But the irony here is twofold: Jesus was the very Lord and Redeemer of Israel spoken of in the passage in Deuteronomy. And, tragically, generations of innocent Jews have been burdened unfairly with blame for Jesus' death, which has been heaped upon them for centuries.

Historically speaking, the cry of the Jewish assembly as reported in Matthew 27:25 has been the source of much terrible treatment of the Jewish people. Nonetheless, neither this passage nor any other justifies unrighteous, inhuman treatment of any member of our Heavenly Father's family. It was not the Jewish people who crucified the Savior but individual evil men. Jesus was a Jew, and so were the apostles and almost every other member of the early Church up to the time of the first mission to the Gentiles during the ministry of Paul of Tarsus. As one Book of Mormon prophet declared, we ought to thank the Jews: "Do [the Gentiles] remember the travails, and the labors, and the pains of the Jews, and their diligence unto me, in bringing forth salvation unto the Gentiles?" (2 Nephi 29:4).

Of course, it is true that many bore responsibility for the Crucifixion, as the scriptures teach, including Herod, Pontius Pilate, and certain other Gentiles, members of the Jerusalem community, and, above all, the Jewish rulers and chief priests of the people. As the early apostles Peter and John said: "The kings of the earth stood up, and the rulers were gathered together against the Lord, and against his Christ. For of a truth against thy holy child Jesus, whom thou hast anointed, both Herod, and Pontius Pilate, with the Gentiles, and the people of Israel, were gathered together" (Acts 4:26–27).

No amount of hand washing could absolve Pilate of responsibility for Jesus' execution; he had the power and the opportunity to stop the illegal and immoral proceedings, but he did not—even though, as I believe, he knew Jesus was the Christ. Elder Neal A. Maxwell declared: "Pilate sought to refuse responsibility for deciding about Christ, but Pilate's hands were never dirtier than just after he had washed them" ("Why Not Now?" 13). In a perceptive comment about Pilate that teaches us the most important lesson of this episode for our own lives, President Spencer W. Kimball asked: "Could the Lord forgive Pilate? Certainly he could not without Pilate's repentance. Did Pilate repent? We do not know what Pilate did after the scripture drops him. He had a desire to favor the Savior. He did not display full courage in resisting the pressures of the people. . . . We leave Pilate to the Lord as we do all other sinners, but remember that 'to know and not to do' is sin" (*Miracle of Forgiveness*, 167).

In another significant irony of history, a few months after the Crucifixion, the same Jewish leaders who had deliberately provoked the early-morning mob to cry for the Savior's blood to be upon them became indignant over the apostles' eyewitness testimony and powerful preaching. They forgot the facts surrounding Jesus' condemnation and accused the apostles, saying, "Ye have filled Jerusalem with your doctrine, and intend to bring this man's blood upon us" (Acts 5:28). Indeed!

SCOURGING

After Pilate's ceremony of self-absolution, Jesus was turned over to the torture of scourging, followed by mocking and more abuse inflicted by soldiers of the governor. Though Luke omits these horrors from his record, and John presents a slightly different chronology, there can be no doubt that these tortures exacted a terrible physical toll from the Savior. Scourging was a legal preliminary to every Roman execution, and prisoners sometimes died from it alone.

The usual instrument delivering the punishment was a short whip (*flagrum*, or *flagellum*) having a wooden handle with several single strands or braided leather thongs that had a lead ball attached to each end. Sometimes pieces of glass or chunks of bone were woven into the thongs. The victim was stripped of all clothing and tied by his wrists to an upright post or pillar. The feet would be dangling and the skin on the back and buttocks stretched tight. The back, buttocks, and back of the legs were flogged with extreme force either by two soldiers (*lictors*) taking turns or by one scourger who alternated positions to get at both halves of the victim's back. The first blows of the thongs cut through the skin only. But subsequent blows cut deeper and deeper into the subcutaneous tissue. The lead balls at the ends of the thongs first produced deep bruises, and then open wounds as the blows were repeated (Davis, "Physician Testifies about Crucifixion," 37).

When the Roman soldiers repeatedly struck the victim's back with full force, the flesh would be torn away in chunks. As the flogging continued, the lacerations would "tear into the underlying skeletal muscles and produce quivering ribbons of bleeding flesh" (Edwards et al., "Physical Death of Jesus Christ," 1457). The number of lashes was supposed to be limited to thirty-nine, according to Jewish law. Deuteronomy 25:3 states that if a guilty man deserves to be beaten, he must not be given more than forty lashes. Later rabbinic law prescribed thirty-nine—"forty stripes save one," as the apostle Paul writes in 2 Corinthians 11:24. This regulation "set a fence around the Torah," as the rabbis said, or, in other words, officially prevented zealous administrators from overstepping the bounds of the Mosaic law. Whether the Roman soldiers exceeded the prescribed number of lashes is unknown, but after his flogging the half-fainting Jesus was untied, slumping to the stone pavement made slippery with his own blood (Davis, "Physician Testifies about Crucifixion," 37).

It was not uncommon for scourging victims to die from lacerated arteries or from extreme shock as a result of trauma to the kidneys or other organs. The severity of the scourging depended on the disposition of the lictors, but the practice was intended to bring the victim to a condition just short of death. The extent of shock and blood loss undoubtedly determined the length of time the victim could survive on the cross. The severity of the scourging Jesus received is not discussed in the four Gospel accounts, but some scholars are convinced that it was particularly harsh in his case (Edwards et al., "Physical Death of Jesus Christ," 1457 58).

Scourging was a brutal, bloody business. But, then again, so was the whole atoning act of our Lord—from Gethsemane through Golgotha. He endured it for the whole human family collectively, as well as for each human being individually and personally. In this regard, the words of President James E. Faust remain forever etched in my mind: "In the words of the hymn, 'Let me not forget, O Savior, / Thou didst bleed and die for me.' I wonder how many drops were shed for me" ("Atonement: Our Greatest Hope," 3).

It has been said that Pilate was trying to create compassion for Jesus as a result of the terrible scourging. But if he was, it did not work. In fact, it may have had the opposite effect on the minds of bloodthirsty leaders who would have revelled in the increasing intensity of the Savior's physical suffering. Certainly, the scene of the Savior's scourging points out another great irony of this situation, as Elder James E. Talmage notes: "Pilate seems to have counted on the pitiful sight of the scourged and bleeding Christ to soften the hearts of the maddened Jews. But the effect failed. Think of the awful fact—a heathen, a pagan, who knew not God, pleading with the priests and people of Israel for the life of their Lord and King!" (*Jesus the Christ*, 598).

The scourging was undoubtedly accomplished at the Praetorium, but Matthew and Mark describe the ensuing mocking by the soldiers as a separate action within the judgment hall.

> Then the soldiers of the governor took Jesus into the common hall, and gathered unto him the whole band of soldiers.
>
> And they stripped him, and put on him a scarlet robe.
>
> And when they had platted a crown of thorns, they put it upon his head, and a reed in his right hand: and they bowed the knee before him, and mocked him, saying, Hail, King of the Jews!

> And they spit upon him, and took the reed, and
> smote him on the head. (Matthew 27:27–30)

The cohort of Roman soldiers in the Praetorium was a large one, perhaps as many as six hundred men—the whole Jerusalem garrison. They were an elite military unit serving under the command of the Roman governor, commissioned to keep the peace in one of the most volatile regions of the empire. Because Jews were exempted from military service in Palestine, all the soldiers must have been Gentiles. At least some of these soldiers were likely part of the arresting party who had seized Jesus the night before in Gethsemane. Many in the cohort had undoubtedly gathered to watch the mocking and abuse, which their comrades knew how to dish out so effectively. One author has written that "Pilate's orders were to scourge and crucify Jesus, but the cruel mockery they heaped upon Him reveals their own wickedness" (MacArthur, *Murder of Jesus*, 190). If not outright wickedness, certainly the soldiers' actions highlight the harshness or brutality of Roman military life.

The mockery continued as the soldiers made a great spectacle of clothing their Prisoner in a robe whose color signified royalty. The "scarlet robe" of the King James Version (Matthew 27:28) is changed in the Joseph Smith Translation to "purple robe" (Matthew 27:30), thus matching Mark's and John's descriptions (Mark 15:17; John 19:5). Purple was the color of royalty, but its use in this case was no compliment. The Roman soldiers must have seen a great joke in a lowly provincial Jew from Galilee, beaten within an inch of his life, who claimed to be the King of the Jewish nation. In fact, the soldiers' humiliating actions mocked both Jesus' true royalty and his true divinity. And still his suffering was far from over. "It seemed as if the whole world was against Jesus. Jews and Gentiles alike were now willfully, even gleefully, participating in His murder, determined to see Him die in the most agonizing way possible. A catalogue of the pains of crucifixion would fill an entire volume" (MacArthur, *Murder of Jesus*, 190).

The apostle John records that after Jesus was scourged and mocked, Pilate made one more attempt to secure Jesus' release. But when he heard the Jews cry out that if he let Jesus go, he was no friend of Caesar, Pilate could no longer resist their incessant demands. He had to issue his final order.

> Pilate therefore went forth again, and saith unto them, Behold, I bring him forth to you, that ye may know that I find no fault in him.
>
> Then came Jesus forth, wearing the crown of thorns, and the purple robe. And Pilate saith unto them, Behold the man!
>
> And from thenceforth Pilate sought to release him: but the Jews cried out, saying, If thou let this man go, thou art not Caesar's friend: whosoever maketh himself a king speaketh against Caesar.
>
> When Pilate therefore heard that saying, he brought Jesus forth, and sat down in the judgment seat in a place that is called the Pavement, but in the Hebrew, Gabbatha. . . .
>
> But they cried out, Away with him, away with him, crucify him. Pilate saith unto them, Shall I crucify your King? The chief priests answered, We have no king but Caesar.
>
> Then delivered he him therefore unto them to be crucified. (John 19: 4–5, 12–13, 15–16)

Amazingly, not only were the Jewish leaders guilty of murdering their true God and King, they were now guilty of abandoning their own traditional statements about God actually being their King, for the sake of their premeditated scheme. But even more stunning than Jewish antagonism toward Jesus is the way the Savior faced up to all that befell him. To think of the God of the universe battered, bruised, dehydrated, exhausted, stripped, and bleeding in front of a taunting crowd is almost more than we can allow ourselves to ponder. His physical suffering is incomprehensible. Not only was he flogged to the point of collapse but he was stripped again, dressed in a robe of mock royalty, spat upon, made to hold a wooden stick in his right hand as a scepter, and beaten on the head after the crown of thorns had been placed on top, thus driving the thorns deeper into his scalp.

The Roman emperor, Caesar, wore a crown made from a laurel wreath; the crown of thorns was undoubtedly a sadistic play on that practice. Many varieties of thorns grow in the Holy Land in modern times, which help us visualize the scene involving the Savior. It is possible his cruel crown that fateful Friday morning was made out of the gruesome inch-long thorns seen occasionally in religious souvenir shops in the Holy Land. In addition, the purple robe being torn from his back would have caused Jesus more pain and fresh bleeding because clots of blood from the scourging would have begun to adhere to the robe (Davis, "Physician Testifies about Crucifixion," 37). How could any human being fail to be moved by such a scene?

One suspects that Jesus was able to endure all of this patiently because his mind and heart were focused on his Father and his Father's will. He knew his Father loved him and that this was what his Father wanted him to do in order to ransom all of his Father's family. Like the firstborn in Israelite society, who was given a double portion of the inheritance to rescue the family and help family members out of their difficulties, Jesus, the firstborn of all our Heavenly Father's spirit children, used all of his strength, all of his physical, emotional, mental, and spiritual reserves, to rescue his Father's family. He was draining the dregs of the bitter cup once again so that none of his brothers and sisters would have to. And even though he had life in himself—that is, he had the power to give up his life of his own accord, to determine the time of his own decease, or to continue to live (John 10:18)—he was quickly reaching his extremity as he stood before his mockers and abusers after his scourging. Only his great reservoirs of strength and superior endowments of power were seeing him through.

There are lessons in this for all of us. First, we are asked by the same Savior who suffered his own tribulations patiently to "be patient in tribulation until I come" (D&C 54:10) and to "continue in patience until ye are perfected" (D&C 67:13). Patience is the pattern of Christlike behavior. It is the highest standard. He showed us the way. He really is the way, the truth, and the life. Given what the Savior endured in patience, we cannot say anything to him about life's unfairness or frustrations that he does not already know by his own experience. Patience is required of all, even the greatest of all. Elder Bruce R. McConkie taught: "To fill the full measure and purpose of our mortal probation, *we must have patience.* This mortal existence is the Lord's sifting sphere, the time when we are subject to trials, testing, and tribulations. Future rewards will be based on our *patient* endurance of all things" (*Mormon Doctrine,* 557; emphasis added).

President John Taylor taught a profound lesson about the importance of submitting patiently to whatever God sees fit to inflict upon us in this schooling process we call mortality. "I have seen men tempted so sorely that finally they would say, 'I'll be damned if I'll stand it any longer,' Well, you will be damned if you do not" (*Journal of Discourses*, 22:318). On the other hand, we may take great comfort in the words of Elder James E. Talmage: "No pang that is suffered by man or woman upon the earth will be without its compensating effect . . . if it be met with patience" (quoted in Kimball, *Faith Precedes the Miracle*, 98).

Second, in order for us to be able to endure all things patiently, we must build up reservoirs of strength and seek endowments of power just as the Savior did in order to get us through the wrenching circumstances of life. An important source of strength and power comes to us from the endowment, or rich gift, given in our temples. Elder Robert D. Hales said:

> In our day, the steadying arm of the Lord reaches us through the ordinances of His holy temples. Said the Prophet Joseph to the early Saints in Nauvoo, "You need an endowment, brethren, in order that you may be prepared and able to overcome all things." How right he was! Being blessed with the temple covenants and endowed with power made it possible for the Latter-day Saints to endure tribulation with faith. At the end of her own pioneer journey, Sarah Rich recorded, "If it had not been for the faith and knowledge that was bestowed upon us in that temple . . . our journey would have been like . . . taking a leap in the dark. ("Faith through Tribulation Brings Peace and Joy," 17)

All of us will have challenging circumstances to pass through in life. The Lord himself will reach out and tug at our very heartstrings, and if we cannot submit patiently to his molding and shaping, we will not be fit for his kingdom. Sometimes we may think that his molding and shaping are more than we can handle or that they are not worth the pain. Nevertheless, we may take comfort in knowing that even for God, the greatest of all, a crown of thorns had to precede his crown of glory. And it is precisely because Jesus experienced the crown of thorns that he has the knowledge and power to wipe away all our tears. Of those who are exalted in God's kingdom, John the Revelator wrote:

> And I said unto him, Sir, thou knowest. And he said to me, These are they which came out of great tribulation, and have washed their robes, and made them white in the blood of the Lamb.
>
> Therefore are they before the throne of God, and serve him day and night in his temple: and he that sitteth on the throne shall dwell among them.
>
> They shall hunger no more, neither thirst any more; neither shall the sun light on them, nor any heat.
>
> For the Lamb which is in the midst of the throne shall feed them, and shall lead them unto living fountains of waters: and God shall wipe away all tears from their eyes. (Revelation 7:14–17)

The image of someone wiping away the tears of another connotes profound tenderness. For me, it conjures up images of a loving parent easing the pains of an injured child. Perhaps the Lord intended to evoke such thoughts when he inspired his apostle John to use the language found in Revelation. All of us are children of God, and all of us are injured in many ways as a result of mortality. The Lord's concern for each of us is individual and personal: His ministrations are intimate, he always takes into consideration our needs and desires, and he knows us by name, as the scriptures demonstrate. It is no small thing for the Lord to promise that he will dry *all* our tears. The price for that power was Gethsemane and Golgotha.

And when they had mocked him, they took off the purple from him, and put his own clothes on him, and led him out to crucify him.

And they compel one Simon a Cyrenian, who passed by, coming out of the country, the father of Alexander and Rufus, to bear his cross.

And they bring him unto the place Golgotha, which is, being interpreted, The place of a skull.

MARK 15:20–22

And there followed him a great company of people, and of women, which also bewailed and lamented him.

But Jesus turning unto them said, Daughters of Jerusalem, weep not for me, but weep for yourselves, and for your children.

For, behold, the days are coming, in the which they shall say, Blessed are the barren, and the wombs that never bare, and the paps which never gave suck.

Then shall they begin to say to the mountains, Fall on us; and to the hills, Cover us.

For if they do these things in a green tree, what shall be done in the dry?

And there were also two other, malefactors, led with him to be put to death.

And when they were come to the place, which is called Calvary, there they crucified him, and the malefactors, one on the right hand, and the other on the left.

LUKE 23:27–33

CHAPTER 8

The Way of the Cross

After Jesus had been made sufficient sport of, to the enjoyment of the taunting and jeering crowd, the Roman soldiers took from him their mock royal robe and, in deference to Jewish custom, put his own clothes back on him (Matthew 27:31). In other cultures the victim was usually left naked. Jesus was then forced to carry his own cross and was led away from the judgment hall with two thieves to the place where the crucifixions were to be carried out (Luke 23:32).

It has been argued, and probably rightly, that the cross Jesus carried (Matthew 27:32; Mark 15:21; Luke 23:26) was not the entire Latin cross as traditionally portrayed. Rather, it was likely only the crossbar, or *patibulum*, which would have been a heavy piece of wood (probably olive) weighing about 75 to 125 pounds and capable of being fastened to a vertical pole or beam. An important ancient source for crucifixion practices refers to the crossbar being carried by the victim through the city beyond the gate (Plautus, *Braggart Warrior*, 161). The Savior's patibulum would have been placed across the nape of his neck, balanced along his shoulders, and tied to both arms (Edwards et al., "Physical Death," 1459). Because crucifixion practices in the ancient world varied according to region and time, it has also been argued that Jesus could have carried the whole cross, either a T-shaped cross or the more familiar Latin cross (†). The writers of the Gospels use the term *stauros* (Greek, "cross"), which does not clarify the picture very much. Whatever Jesus carried, he bore a tremendous physical load, in addition to the mental, emotional, and spiritual burdens of the whole experience.

No executions were performed within the city walls (Numbers 15:35; 1 Kings 21:13; Acts 7:58). The procession to the site of crucifixion outside the city was led by a centurion and at least a quaternion (four soldiers), according to John 19:23. One of the soldiers carried a sign (*titulus*), on which the condemned man's name and crime were written. The titulus would later be fastened to the top of the cross.

Beyond Jerusalem's walls would have been upright wooden posts, or poles (Latin, *stipes*), upon which a victim's patibulum would be fastened. The practice of crucifixion probably began in Persia, where the victim was tied to or impaled upon a tree or upright post to keep his feet from touching the ground so that the torturous process of crucifixion could do its ghastly work of slow death by asphyxiation. It is likely that the upright post, or stipes, to which the Savior's patibulum was fastened was a tree whose branches had been cut off.

The apostle Paul seems to refer to this in his discussion of Christ's many-faceted redemptive act: "Christ hath redeemed us from the curse of the law, being made a curse for us: for it is written, Cursed is every one that hangeth on a tree" (Galatians 3:13). Paul was quoting Deuteronomy 21:23, which may be viewed as a prophetic reference made by Moses to the future crucifixion of the Savior (the book of Deuteronomy consists of Moses' final three sermons). This Deuteronomic passage was used by later Jews to emphasize the abhorrent nature of crucifixion as a way to die—"cursed is every one that hangeth on a tree." Thus, Paul was saying that Jesus redeemed us from the impossibility of being perfected through the Mosaic law by being crucified on a tree, an abhorrent form of death.

The apostle Peter also refers to the tree as the method of Jesus' crucifixion. He speaks of our Savior as the One "who his own self bare our sins in his own body on the tree, that we, being dead to sins, should live unto righteousness: by whose stripes ye were healed" (1 Peter 2:24).

As Jesus made his way from the Praetorium to the place of crucifixion, it appears that the cumulative effects of the events of the previous twenty-four hours had so weakened the Savior that he stumbled or collapsed. Clearly he needed help carrying his cross. The soldiers compelled one Simon of Cyrene, "who passed by, coming out of the country, the father of Alexander and Rufus, to bear his cross" (Mark 15:21). Luke tells us that Simon followed behind the Savior, now carrying the burden that had caused the Savior to stumble (Luke 23:26).

The Savior's collapse is understandable. His redemptive suffering and agony of atonement had caused him to sweat blood in Gethsemane. He was arrested, treated like a criminal, and marched up to the palace of the high priests, then to Pilate, then to Herod, and then back to Pilate. He had been beaten, held without sleep all night, beaten again, stripped, scourged, beaten once more, stripped again, and mocked. Is it any wonder he stumbled under the weight of the cross?

Also understandable is the impatience of the Roman

soldiers who, responding to Jewish impetus, wanted to get this crucifixion over with. Jesus was slowing things down, and the law outlined in Deuteronomy 21:22–23 was undoubtedly on everyone's mind: "And if a man have committed a sin worthy of death, and he be to be put to death, and thou hang him on a tree: His body shall not remain all night upon the tree, but thou shalt in any wise bury him that day." John also indicates that the Jews were anxious that the body of Jesus "not remain on the cross" (John 19:31). The sooner the crucifixion could be accomplished, the better—from their perspective.

THE LESSON OF SIMON OF CYRENE

We know little about the man whom the Roman soldiers picked out of the crowd and "compelled" to carry the Savior's cross (Matthew 27:32). He is one of nine characters in the New Testament named Simon. The Gospel of Mark says he was a passerby, on his way into Jerusalem from the country (Mark 15:21), undoubtedly to participate in the Passover feast. The Mosaic law required all males of the covenant to appear before the Lord three times a year in the place that He chose. The three occasions were the Feast of Unleavened Bread (or Passover), the Feast of Weeks (or Pentecost), and the Feast of Tabernacles (Deuteronomy 16:16; Exodus 23:14–17). By this time in Israel's history, the place chosen was understood to be the Temple in Jerusalem.

Simon seems to have had no previous association with Jesus. His meeting with the Savior was a seeming chance encounter, not planned by Simon, at any rate. But he was not an idle rabble-rouser and not part of the crowd in attendance at the Savior's trial for the purpose of mocking him. Simon was from Cyrene, a leading town of Libya in North Africa, west of Egypt, with a large Jewish population. That Jews from Cyrene went to Jerusalem regularly to keep the law of pilgrimage festivals as prescribed in the Torah may be inferred from a later New Testament account that indicates representatives from Cyrene were present in the capital city on the day of Pentecost, fifty days after Passover (Acts 2:10). We can imagine Simon standing in the Jerusalem thoroughfare simply out of curiosity about the spectacle taking place that Friday morning as Passover approached.

Mark adds a further detail, unrelated to anything immediately connected with Jesus' trial but which seems to indicate that Simon's service proved to be of eternal consequence for Simon himself. Mark says, without explanation, that Simon was "the father of Alexander and Rufus" (Mark 15:21). Was this information mentioned at this point because an important connection would be understood by Mark's readers in the early Church? Apparently so.

In Romans 16:13 the apostle Paul mentions Rufus, "chosen in the Lord," as well as Rufus's mother, who was also a mother (nurturer) to Paul himself. As has been suggested by others, it is quite possible that the gospel came into Simon's life as well as to his family as a result of his seemingly chance encounter with the Savior of the world at the very moment He was on His way to Golgotha to complete the atoning event that is at the core of our Father's plan for all creation. The power of the event in which Simon had a role, and which he later came to comprehend, ultimately resulted in his own conversion as well as that of his wife, his sons, and possibly future generations. Mark, who mentioned Simon's sons, was a companion and scribe to Peter, the chief apostle, when Peter was in the twilight of his ministry in Rome. There he recounted details that Mark used to write his Gospel. Rufus and Alexander would have been known to the early Church, and Mark was providing details about their family association. Thus, Simon may not have been happy at first about having to carry the cross of a convicted enemy of Rome and the Jewish people, but the path to Golgotha seems to have become the path to eternal life for him and his family.

Archaeologists working in Jerusalem believe that a group of ossuaries (stone boxes for the burial of human bones) discovered in 1941 belonged to the family of Simon of Cyrene. Ossuaries were widely used in Jerusalem in the first century after Christ. The Simon family ossuaries were found in a Kidron Valley tomb and bear names pointing "to a family that originated in Cyrenaica [Cyrene]; one inscription bears the name Alexander, a name rare among Jews at the time; he is identified as the Son of Simon" (Powers, "Treasures in the Storeroom," 51). What better location for Simon and his family to be buried than in the place where they found salvation.

The story of Simon of Cyrene has an important application to our lives. Like Simon, we never know when some act of service, even some unintended act of consideration, will return to us many fold. The scriptures teach this lesson profoundly: "Cast thy bread upon the waters: for thou shalt find it after many days" (Ecclesiastes 11:1). This verse urges us to do good to those around us, to give help to those who need it, and it promises that rewards will come back to bless us. One small real-life example will suffice.

Years ago I was serving as a bishop in a city where a Latter-day Saint temple was nearing completion. Simply because I was the current bishop, I received two admission passes to the celestial room to witness the dedicatory service. My wife suggested that the passes really ought to go to a couple who had worked hard throughout the previous several years to ensure the timely opening of the temple rather than me, since I had only been called as bishop after the planning and construction of the new edifice were well along. Having been raised in the city where a temple was finally becoming a reality after long years of waiting, I really wanted to be in the celestial room for the dedication. In the end I decided my wife was right (as she usually is), and besides, two passes would not allow us to have our two eligible children with us to witness the dedication in the celestial room. We desired above all else to participate in the proceedings together as a family, and so I gave the two passes to the eminently deserving couple.

On the day of the dedication, our family entered the temple with great anticipation. We sat together in one of the rooms of the temple, ready to participate via closed circuit television with those in the celestial room. Then one of the stake presidents in the region who was acting as an usher, but whom I had never met, came into our room. He looked around, walked directly up to me, and asked how many members of my family were there. I answered "Four," and he responded, "Please come with me." He led our little family to the celestial room to enjoy the dedicatory service in the presence of the Brethren and our stake choir as well. There were exactly four vacant seats in the celestial room that morning. With overflowing hearts my wife and I turned to each other and said, almost in unison, "Cast your bread upon the waters, and it will come back many fold." What added to our joy was seeing in the celestial room the couple to whom we had given the original tickets. Everyone was blessed that day but no one more than I for the opportunity of witnessing a demonstration of the principle that also seems to have blessed Simon of Cyrene.

A FINAL WARNING

The Gospel of Luke alone records that after Simon was forced to carry the cross, Jesus turned to the "great company of people" that had been following him and pointedly delivered his last public message on the road to Golgotha (Luke 23:27). Luke is careful to tell us that the group was composed of women who had been mourning and wailing for Him in their traditional manner. In fact, Luke seems to have had a greater interest in the women who had associated themselves with Jesus from the beginning of his ministry than the other Gospel writers. He alone points out that as the Savior traveled from one town and village to another, many women traveled with him and the Twelve and "ministered unto him [Jesus] of their substance" (Luke 8:3; see also vv. 1–2). Luke's witness helps us to see that faithful women have always played an important role in the Lord's Church. From the earliest period onward, they have ministered to those who needed support, even out of their own means.

Now approaching Golgotha, Jesus, ever the Master Teacher, turned to some of these same women, as we suppose, and spoke this warning: "Daughters of Jerusalem, weep not for me, but weep for yourselves, and for your children. For, behold, the days are coming, in the which they shall say, Blessed are the barren, and the wombs that never bare, and the paps which never gave suck. Then shall they begin to say to the mountains, Fall on us; and to the hills, Cover us. For if they do these things in a green tree, what shall be done in the dry?" (Luke 23:28–31).

This warning was of impending disaster of the greatest

proportions. In Jewish society the birth of a child was understood to be among the highest blessings that God could bestow upon a woman and a people. It was a tangible symbol of hope in the future. On the other hand, the greatest curse for women in Old Testament times was barrenness and miscarriage (Hosea 9:14). By quoting Hosea 10:8 ("they shall say to the mountains, Cover us; and to the hills, Fall on us") to those who were following him, the Savior was prophesying that things in the future would get so ugly, so terrible, for the Jewish nation and the people in Jerusalem that women would not want to bring children into the world to experience such horrors. Rather, they would wish for themselves to be annihilated without the blessing of motherhood. They would gladly accept escape through natural calamity rather than have to endure the kind of suffering that was to come. The Joseph Smith Translation of Luke 23:32 tells us that this prophecy of future devastation was also meant to include the desolation of the Gentiles as well as the scattering of Israel.

In the last part of his warning, Jesus explicitly tied the disasters of the future to the leaders' treatment of himself. He himself is the Green Tree referred to in the warning; he is the Life and the Light, the giver of enlightenment and all good things, the provider of the very environment in which righteousness could most easily flourish. Jesus was saying, in effect, that if the Jewish nation could carry out such wickedness (as the Crucifixion) when the very Son of God was among them *and* at a time when they could have flourished religiously, what would happen to them after the Green Tree was killed and gone and only "the withered branches and dried trunk of apostate Judaism" remained? (Talmage, *Jesus the Christ*, 654). What would happen to Judaism after disaster overtook the Jews?

Virtually the same image was invoked when the martyrdoms of the Prophet Joseph Smith and his brother, the Patriarch Hyrum Smith, were announced: "If the fire can scathe a green tree for the glory of God, how easy it will burn up the dry trees to purify the vineyard of corruption" (D&C 135:6).

Little did the Jewish people of the Savior's day realize that in only forty short years their world would be devastated—changed forever. By A.D. 70 the Romans would lay siege to Jerusalem and ultimately obliterate the Temple. Things would indeed get so bad, as the Jewish historian Josephus would later report, that the besieged inhabitants of Jerusalem, even the women, would one day resort to cannibalism. "Mothers snatched food from their children's mouths and one mother roasted her own son to survive. The time foreseen by Jesus when she who had no child or babe at the breast would bless herself, or when one might call upon mountains to fall and bring merciful release, was at hand. Women of Jerusalem were bitterly weeping for themselves" (Peterson and Tate, *Pearl of Great Price*, 190; see Josephus, *Wars of the Jews*, 6.3.4).

The Temple itself was destroyed on the ninth of Av (August 28), A.D. 70. "As the Temple burned, frenzy gripped both attackers and defenders. Roman shock troops burst through, and Titus was able to dash into the Temple just long enough for a brief look; then heat forced him out. His soldiers continued burning whatever could be kindled, and killing all they could reach, whether combatants, women, or children. Many Jews flung themselves into the fire and perished with their Temple. Others, hiding in corners, were burned to death as Roman torches set new fires" (Klein and Klein, *Temple beyond Time*, 112).

The final scenes of Jerusalem's total devastation a month

later, on a September day in A.D. 70, are reported with equal vividness: "Pouring into the alleys, sword in hand, [the soldiers] massacred indiscriminately all whom they met, *and burnt the houses with all who had taken refuge within.* Often in the course of their raids, on entering the houses for loot, they would find whole families dead and the rooms filled with victims of the famine. . . . Running everyone through who fell in their way, they choked the alleys with corpses and deluged the whole city with blood, insomuch that many of the fires were extinguished by the gory stream. Towards the evening they ceased slaughtering, but when night fell the fire gained the mastery" (Josephus, *Wars of the Jews,* 6.8–10, quoted in Avigad, *Discovering Jerusalem,* 137).

Such are the scenes the Savior foresaw when he prophesied to the people of their impending doom even as he himself approached his own death at Golgotha. Ironically, the Jewish inhabitants of Jerusalem that Friday morning had as much regard for the possibility that their great city could be destroyed as had Laman and Lemuel six hundred years before (1 Nephi 2:13). To them it was impossible. But obliviousness did not forestall the destruction, either in Lehi's time or a few decades after the Savior's. Of the fulfillment of the Savior's prophecy, Elder Bruce R. McConkie wrote:

> And now the ax was laid at the root of the rotted tree. Jerusalem was to pay the price. Daniel had foretold this hour when desolation, born of abomination and wickedness, would sweep the city. . . . Moses had said the siege would be so severe women would eat their own children. (Deut. 28.) Jesus specified the destruction would come in the days of the disciples.
>
> And come it did, in vengeance, without restraint.

Hunger exceeded human endurance; blood flowed in the streets; destruction made desolate the temple; 1,100,000 Jews were slaughtered; Jerusalem was ploughed as a field; and a remnant of a once mighty nation scattered to the ends of the earth. The Jewish nation died, impaled on Roman spears, at the hands of Gentile overlords. (*Doctrinal New Testament Commentary*, 1:644)

What caused such devastation? Some would argue that the root cause was wickedness of this kind or that—godlessness, conspiracy, murder, brigandage, secret combinations, or the like. It is true that Book of Mormon prophets attributed the fall of their own civilizations to such activity; however, I believe that ultimately Jerusalem and her inhabitants were destroyed because they rejected their true King. Their supreme act of disloyalty was dismissing Jesus' claims to be the long-awaited Messiah, who came to earth to fulfill millennia-old prophecies. The rabbis taught that "all the prophets prophesied only concerning the days of the Messiah" (*Tractate Sanhedrin*, 141), and yet the Fulfillment of those prophecies was put to death in the most ignominious way, crucified between two thieves.

The events of A.D. 70 should have been no surprise to the inhabitants of the Holy City. Jesus had said near the end of his ministry, "Except ye repent, ye shall all likewise perish" (Luke 13:5), and he gave the parable of the fig tree as an illustration: "If it bear fruit, well: and if not, then after that thou shalt cut it down" (Luke 13:9). The image of the fig tree was familiar to the Savior's listeners, for Israel was described as a fig tree in Jewish teachings. And yet, after the Crucifixion, after so many witnesses, Jerusalem's leaders sank deeper into the mire of hatred for Jesus, though they knew the truth, as the book of Acts confirms (Acts 4:1–30; 5:17–33).

The Gospels of Matthew and John report in more or less the same language as the Gospel of Mark that, having delivered his final public warning, Jesus was brought "unto the place Golgotha, which is, being interpreted, The place of a skull" (Mark 15:22; Matthew 27:33; John 19:17). Interestingly, the Joseph Smith Translation changes "skull" to "burial" (JST Mark 15:25). Only the Gospel of Luke calls the site Calvary (Luke 23:33), the Latin equivalent (*calvaria*) of the Aramaic name, *Golgotha*. The four Gospel writers record that at Golgotha the sinless Son of God was crucified between two other men. Luke refers to them as malefactors (criminals), Matthew and Mark call them thieves, and John does not label them. But all the Gospels state explicitly that at Golgotha the Savior of the world was subjected to the slow, agonizing torture of crucifixion, a form of execution that modern, civilized readers can only begin to comprehend.

And when they were come to the place, which is called Calvary, there they crucified him, and the malefactors, one on the right hand, and the other on the left.

Then said Jesus, Father, forgive them; for they know not what they do. And they parted his raiment, and cast lots.

And the people stood beholding. And the rulers also with them derided him, saying, He saved others; let him save himself, if he be Christ, the chosen of God. And the soldiers also mocked him, coming to him, and offering him vinegar, and saying, If thou be the king of the Jews, save thyself.

And a superscription also was written over him in letters of Greek, and Latin, and Hebrew, THIS IS THE KING OF THE JEWS.

And one of the malefactors which were hanged railed on him, saying, If thou be Christ, save thyself and us. But the other answering rebuked him, saying, Dost not thou fear God, seeing thou art in the same condemnation? And we indeed justly; for we receive the due reward of our deeds: but this man hath done nothing amiss.

And he said unto Jesus, Lord, remember me when thou comest into thy kingdom. And Jesus said unto him, Verily I say unto thee, To day shalt thou be with me in paradise.

LUKE 23:33–43

Now there stood by the cross of Jesus his mother, and his mother's sister, Mary the wife of Cleophas, and Mary Magdalene.

When Jesus therefore saw his mother, and the disciple standing by, whom he loved, he saith unto his mother, Woman, behold thy son!

Then saith he to the disciple, Behold thy mother! And from that hour that disciple took her unto his own home.

JOHN 19:26–27

CHAPTER 9

The Character of Christ

When Jesus, his captors, and the crowd following them reached the area called "The Skull," the actual crucifixion took place. So continued the fulfillment of prophecies long foretold by Israel's ancient prophets. That all of the Lord's prophets spoke of such things is attested by Abinadi:

> For behold, did not Moses prophesy unto them concerning the coming of the Messiah, and that God should redeem his people? Yea, and even all the prophets who have prophesied ever since the world began—have they not spoken more or less concerning these things?
>
> Have they not said that God himself should come down among the children of men, and take upon him the form of man, and go forth in mighty power upon the face of the earth?
>
> Yea, and have they not said also that he should bring to pass the resurrection of the dead, and that he, himself, should be oppressed and afflicted? (Mosiah 13:33–35)

We do not know precisely where Golgotha was located. Despite many paintings over the centuries showing Jesus being crucified on a hill and despite some of our hymns referring to the "hill" of Calvary, nothing in scripture indicates that his crucifixion occurred on a hill. It could have taken place alongside the main road just outside Jerusalem's walls, to show everyone who passed by that the Romans were in charge and that anyone who defied their authority could meet a similar ignominious death and themselves be thus reviled by future onlookers. The Roman writer Quintilian (ca. A.D. 35–95) recorded: "Whenever we crucify the guilty, the most crowded roads are chosen, where the most people can see and be moved by this fear. For penalties relate not so much to retribution as to their exemplary effect" (*Decl.* 274, as cited in *Anchor Bible Dictionary*, 1:1208).

Two principal sites have been considered as possibilities for the exact spot where the Savior's crucifixion occurred: the Church of the Holy Sepulchre, now located inside the old city of Jerusalem, and Gordon's Calvary, commonly known as the Garden Tomb, north of Damascus Gate. Both sites have pros and cons, but as I view the evidence, I am inclined to regard as a primary factor the important geographical symbolism behind the ancient Mosaic requirement that all animal sacrifices and offerings of the Tabernacle and Temple be killed "on the side of the altar northward before the Lord" (Leviticus 1:11). In other words, from Mosaic times onward, the animal sacrifices that constituted the most important element of the various sanctuary offerings (burnt, peace, sin, etc.), and which symbolized the great and last sacrifice of the Son of God (Alma 34:13–14), were always slaughtered north of the altars of both the Tabernacle in the wilderness and, later, the Temple. Therefore, wherever we look for the precise location of Golgotha, symbolic necessity dictates that we look north of the great altar of the Temple at Jerusalem. This geographic symbolism is simply one of the many foreshadowings of the Lord's crucifixion found in ancient Israelite religion.

THE CRUELTIES OF CRUCIFIXION

Crucifixion was one of the most brutal forms of execution ever invented. "No word can be found adequate to describe so monstrous a proceeding," wrote the Roman statesman Cicero (quoted in McConkie, *Doctrinal New Testament Commentary,* 1:814). It is instructive to note that our English word *excruciating* ("unbearably intense pain, agony, torture") derives from the same Latin root as does *crucifixion* (*crucis*). Though the practice of crucifixion was not original to the Romans, they adopted and perfected it into a form of capital punishment that brought about an agonizingly slow death with the greatest possible pain and suffering. Sometimes a victim lived on for days—with ever-increasing torment. The victim was stripped naked, nailed to the cross (not tied, as in some earlier cultures, such as Egypt) by driving spikes through the victim's outstretched hands or wrists as well as through his feet and then into the wooden cross. The nails were expertly pounded in to avoid breaking bones and penetrating major blood vessels so the victim would not bleed to death. But the driven nails would crush or sever important nerves in the wrists, producing "excruciating bolts of fiery pain in both arms . . . [and] paralysis of a portion of the hand, [while] ischemic contractures and impalement of various ligaments by the iron spike might produce a clawlike grasp" (Edwards et al., "Physical Death of Jesus Christ," 1460).

When the victim was thrown to the ground on his back so that the executioner could stretch out the victim's arms against the patibulum, or crossbar, and drive the nails through his hands and wrists and feet, the wounds from the preceding scourging would likely be torn open again and become contaminated from the dirt on the ground. When the victim was lifted into place on the *stipes* (pole), or tree, the victim's arms would bear the full weight of his body. As the victim sagged and more weight was put on the wrists, excruciating pain would shoot along the fingers and up the arms. "To relieve some of the pain in the hands, wrists, and arms, the victim would push down on his feet to raise himself up with the result that searing pain would shoot up the legs from the nail-wounds in the feet. At some point, waves of cramps would sweep over the muscles of the legs and feet, causing throbbing pain as well as the inability to push upward and relieve the pain and pressure in the arms and wrists. Also, with the arms stretched out on the cross, breathing became increasingly difficult. Air could be drawn into the lungs, but not exhaled and asphyxiation eventually resulted" (Davis, "Physician Testifies about Crucifixion," 39). When the legs of the victim were broken, as reported in John 19:31–33, death resulted much more quickly because of the added shock to the body and, especially, the inability of the victim to raise up his body and stave off asphyxiation.

In 1968 the remains of a man crucified in the first century after Christ were discovered in an ossuary (casket for bones) from an ancient burial site located in present-day north Jerusalem (Giv'at ha-Mivtar). The victim's name, Yehohanan ben Hagkol, was engraved on the ossuary. He seems to have been between twenty-four and twenty-eight years of age. This find was of monumental proportions because it constituted the first and greatest archeological evidence of crucifixion, even though thousands of people were known from literary evidence to have been crucified by the Romans, who usually reserved the practice for male slaves, prisoners, and rebels.

In the ossuary of Yehohanan was a heel bone that still had the four-and-one-half-inch-long crucifixion nail embedded in it. Significantly, scholarly analysis indicates that the feet of this condemned man were nailed laterally, and thus separately, to the upright part of the cross, so that he straddled it. Furthermore, when this victim's feet were nailed to the cross, an olive wood plaque had been placed between the head of the spike and the foot to prevent the victim from pulling free of the spike (Zias and Sekeles, "Crucified Man from Giv'at ha-Mivtar," 190). The crucifixion of the Savior may have proceeded in a similar fashion.

Elder Bruce R. McConkie graphically describes some of the physical aspects of crucifixion:

> A death by crucifixion seems to include all that pain and death can have of the horrible and ghastly—dizziness, cramp, thirst, starvation, sleeplessness, traumatic fever, tetanus, publicity of shame, long continuance of torment, horror of anticipation, mortification of untended wounds, all intensified just up to the point at which they can be endured at all, but all stopping just short of the point which would give to the sufferer the relief of unconsciousness. The unnatural position made every movement painful; the lacerated veins and crushed tendons throbbed with incessant anguish; the wounds, inflamed by exposure, gradually gangrened; the arteries, especially of the head and stomach, became swollen and oppressed with surcharged blood; and, while each variety of misery went on gradually increasing,

there was added to them the intolerable pang of a burning and raging thirst. Such was the death to which Christ was doomed. (*Doctrinal New Testament Commentary,* 1:816)

It was not uncommon for the dying and helpless victim on the cross to be plagued by insects that would light upon or burrow into his flesh. After the victim died, his body was often left on the cross to decompose and be eaten by scavenging birds and animals (Edwards et al., "Physical Death of Jesus Christ," 1460).

JESUS ON THE CROSS: PROPHECIES FULFILLED

The Gospel of Mark tells us that the Savior was crucified at nine o'clock in the morning (Mark 15:25). Both Matthew and Mark report that when Jesus reached Golgotha, before he was placed on the cross, he was offered a drink, which he refused. Matthew 27:34 describes the liquid as wine (the Greek *oinos* here is translated as "vinegar" in the King James Version) mixed with gall, while Mark 15:23 says "wine mingled with myrrh." The precise reason for the drink is not made clear in either Gospel. The Babylonian Talmud indicates that wine mixed with frankincense was given to condemned men as a mild analgesic to diminish pain without loss of consciousness, and the drink offered to Jesus is often regarded as having this purpose (see, for example, Davis, "Physician Testifies about Crucifixion," 37). In Jesus' case, some scholars say, the drink was intended to prolong the agony of crucifixion. Others point out that gall is a poison, and its addition to wine would have produced a mildly poisonous substance. Thus, Jesus could have being refusing something that would have made him sick (*Interpreter's Dictionary of the Bible,* s.v. "Gall," 350).

The scriptures do not describe the scene of Jesus being nailed to the cross, but we know that he was stripped of his clothing, as were other crucifixion victims. All four Gospels report that after the soldiers had crucified Jesus, they took his garments and cast lots for ownership because the clothing was valuable (John 19:23–24). In first-century Palestine, Jewish men traditionally wore five pieces of clothing: shoes or sandals, a headdress, an inner tunic, an outer cloak, and a girdle or wide belt. According to Roman custom, these articles became the property of the soldiers performing the crucifixion.

The unnatural and contorted position of the Savior's body nailed on the cross was foreseen by Israel's ancient psalmist. He expressed his graphic prophecy in poetic form: "I am poured out like water, and all my bones are out of joint: my heart is like wax; it is melted in the midst of my bowels" (Psalm 22:14).

It is well known that spikes were driven through the Savior's wrists in addition to the palms of his hands for fear that the weight of his body would cause it to tear away from the cross. Medical authorities attest that it "has been shown that the ligaments and bones of the wrist can support the weight of a body hanging from them, but the palms cannot" (Edwards et al., "Physical Death of Jesus Christ," 1460). The nails driven into the Savior's wrists fastened him securely to the cross and also fulfilled a messianic prophecy of Isaiah, whose graphic imagery resonates deeply with faithful members of the Church:

> And I will clothe him with thy robe, and strengthen him with thy girdle, and I will commit thy government into his hand: and he shall be a father to the inhabitants of Jerusalem, and to the house of Judah.
>
> And the key of the house of David will I lay upon

his shoulder; so he shall open, and none shall shut; and he shall shut, and none shall open.

And I will fasten him as a nail in a sure place; and he shall be for a glorious throne to his father's house.

And they shall hang upon him all the glory of his father's house, the offspring and the issue, all vessels of small quantity, from the vessels of cups, even to all the vessels of flagons.

In that day, saith the Lord of hosts, shall the nail that is fastened in the sure place be removed, and be cut down, and fall; and the burden that was upon it shall be cut off: for the Lord hath spoken it. (Isaiah 22:21–25)

Here Isaiah, whose entire book constitutes a powerful witness of both the first and the second comings of the Messiah, describes the multifaceted role of our Redeemer in the guise of a servant of God named Eliakim (a name that means "God shall cause to rise" and is itself messianic). In one way or another, all the characteristics Isaiah enumerates describe the Lord, Jesus Christ:

1. He would be given the government, or right to rule (v. 21).

2. He would be a father to the house of Judah (v. 21).

3. He would be given "the key of the house of David" (v. 22).

4. He would be fastened to something as "a nail in a sure place" (v. 23).

5. Upon him would be "hung," or placed, the glory of his father's house (v. 24)

6. He would be involved in the removing of the burden associated with "the nail that is fastened in the sure place" (v. 25).

Indeed, this list describes the mission and ministry of Jesus Christ, for by virtue of his mortal mission and atoning sacrifice, he alone fits the characteristics enumerated by Isaiah:

1. He alone possesses "the government"—the power and authority to rule in heaven and on earth—and he will do so at his second coming (D&C 58:22).

2. He is the father, or king, of the Jews (as the title on his cross rightly declared; Matthew 27:37), and he alone is the spiritual father of Israel and of all who obey him (Mosiah 27:25).

3. He alone possesses the "key of the house of David," the symbol of absolute power and authority (both monarchial and priestly) invested in the true Messiah, who descends literally from Israel's greatest monarch, King David (Revelation 3:7).

4. He was in very deed fastened to the cross both *as* and *with* "a nail in a sure place" (Isaiah 22:23).

5. He alone was given his Father's power and glory through divine investiture of authority: "The Father has honored Christ by placing his name upon him, so that he can minister in and through that name as though he were the Father; and thus, so far as power and authority are concerned, his words and acts become and are those of the Father" (Smith, *Doctrines of Salvation,* 1:29–30).

6. He had the glory of his Father's house placed upon him during the last week of his ministry when he referred to the Jerusalem Temple not as "my Father's house" (which he had done at the beginning of his ministry; John 2:16) but rather as "my house" (after his triumphal entry; Matthew 21:13).

7. Last, but not least, he alone is the One who took upon himself the great "burden" referred to by Isaiah, and who

removed that burden from the world when "the nail that was fastened in the sure place was removed" (Isaiah 22:25). In other words, Jesus the Messiah removed from us the burden of physical and spiritual death when he completed the Atonement (that is, after he was removed from the cross, buried, and resurrected).

There is hardly a more powerful image in scripture than the image Isaiah uses of the nail in the sure place. It links the physical act of Christ's crucifixion with the profoundest rituals and remembrances of that act in Latter-day Saint theology and practice.

THE TITLE ON THE CROSS

All four Gospels mention the titulus, or inscription, that was affixed to the cross above Jesus' head. John's account of it is the fullest, attributing the inscription to Pilate, the Roman governor:

> And Pilate wrote a title, and put it on the cross. And the writing was, Jesus of Nazareth the King of the Jews.
>
> This title then read many of the Jews: for the place where Jesus was crucified was nigh to the city: and it was written in Hebrew, and Greek, and Latin.
>
> Then said the chief priests of the Jews to Pilate, Write not, The King of the Jews; but that he said, I am King of the Jews.
>
> Pilate answered, What I have written I have written. (John 19:19–22)

Other ancient texts describe the use of such inscriptions, which announced the official crimes of the condemned and which the convicted was sometimes obliged to wear around his neck until he reached the place of execution. Its use here was clearly intended by Pilate to chide the Jews, for when the chief priests, those most responsible for the Savior's crucifixion, wanted the titulus changed to reflect their charge of blasphemy, Pilate finally showed some backbone and ordered that the inscription stand as originally composed: "What I have written I have written" (John 19:22). Pilate knew not only that Jesus was innocent of any real crime but also that Jesus was who he said he was. Pilate knew the truth. He really knew! (Talmage, *Jesus the Christ*, 657).

Though such inscriptions as the one placed over Jesus' head were intended as a declaration of the condemned man's crimes, ironically Jesus' titulus declared the absolute truth. Jesus was the king of the Jews by lineage and birthright. The Jewish leaders were engulfed in such apostasy that they refused to recognize in Jesus of Nazareth the fulfillment of their own prophecies and traditions. Pilate was engulfed in such concerns about his position that he did not act on the knowledge he possessed.

That the message of the titulus was composed in Hebrew, Greek, and Latin (Luke 23:38) points out the complicated cultural and linguistic situation in Roman Palestine. Latin was the language of the Roman overloads, Greek the lingua franca of the hellenistic world of which Palestine was part, and Hebrew—probably meaning Aramaic—was the common language of the Jews in Jesus' day. Individuals passing the site of crucifixion on that day would have been able to read Jesus' titulus for themselves, no matter what Mediterranean culture they belonged to. In fact, a large proportion of Jews in Jesus' day could read.

John's Gospel contains the fullest account of the scene at

the foot of the cross involving soldiers casting lots for the Savior's clothing as he hung above them (John 19:23–24). John helps us to see how Israel's ancient psalms presented prophecies of the Savior's atoning act. After reporting the actual words of the soldiers, who said, in effect, "Let's not tear the seamless coat; let's decide by lot who will get it," John provides indispensable interpretive commentary that links this event with Psalm 22:18. John declares that the soldiers did what they did "that the scripture might be fulfilled, which saith, They parted my raiment among them, and for my vesture they did cast lots" (John 19:24), an exact quotation of Psalm 22:18.

STATEMENTS FROM THE CROSS

It is at this point in the story that Luke's Gospel places the first of the Savior's seven recorded utterances from the cross, that is, immediately after Luke's brief description of the titulus and right before his mention of the soldiers casting lots for Jesus' raiment. It is instructive to view these statements together, for they teach us much about the Master's last thoughts and feelings. Even today we tend to regard a person's dying declarations with utmost credibility and significance.

1. "Father, forgive them; for they know not what they do" (Luke 23:34).

2. "Verily I say unto thee, To day shalt thou be with me in paradise" (Luke 23:43).

3. "Woman, behold thy son! . . . Behold thy mother!" (John 19:26–27).

4. "My God, my God, why hast thou forsaken me?" (Matthew 27:46; Psalm 22:1).

132

5. "I thirst" (John 19:28).

6. "It is finished" (John 19:30).

7. "Father, into thy hands I commend my spirit" (Luke 23:46; Psalm 31:5).

Perhaps it was the sight of the soldiers' activity at the crucifixion site that prompted the Savior to make his first and probably best known plea: "Father, forgive them; for they know not what they do" (Luke 23:34). No explicit motivation behind the statement is recorded other than the comment about the soldiers casting lots, which Luke describes taking place while Jesus asks for forgiveness for his executioners. Because of its position in the narrative, some confusion has arisen over just who the Savior was asking forgiveness for. The Joseph Smith Translation clarifies this, adding the phrase, "Meaning the soldiers who crucified him" (JST Luke 23:35). Elder Spencer W. Kimball makes this point clearly and teaches us a valuable lesson at the same time:

> When the Lord, in his dying moments, turned to the Father and requested, "Father, forgive them; for they know not what they do" (Luke 23:34), he was referring to the soldiers who crucified him. They acted under the mandate of a sovereign nation. It was the Jews who were guilty of the Lord's death. Again how could he forgive them, or how could his Father forgive them, when they were not repentant. These vicious people who cried, " . . . His blood be on us, and on our children" (Matt. 27:25) had not repented. Those who "reviled him" on Calvary (Matt. 27:39) had not repented. The Jewish leaders who tried Jesus illegally, demanded his crucifixion

from Pilate, and incited the mob to their vilest actions had not repented. Nor had the Roman soldiers who, though no doubt obligated under their military law to crucify Jesus as instructed, were under no compulsion to add the insults and cruelties to which they subjected the Savior prior to his crucifixion. (*Miracle of Forgiveness*, 167)

As Jesus hung on the cross, the Synoptic Gospels report, passersby as well as the members of the gathered crowd mocked and ridiculed him. These included the same ones who engineered the whole conspiracy (the chief priests, scribes, and elders). They not only railed at him and reviled him, wagging their heads as one might do to a fool who had been told better, but also twisted his own words to make those words appear to be the height of foolishness and arrogance. "Thou that destroyest the temple, and buildest it in three days, save thyself" (Matthew 27:40). "He trusted in God; let him deliver him now . . . for he said, I am the Son of God" (Matthew 27:43). "Save thyself, and come down from the cross" (Mark 15:30). "Let Christ the King of Israel descend now from the cross, that we may see and believe" (Mark 15:32). "He saved others; let him save himself, if he be Christ, the chosen of God" (Luke 23:35).

All of these statements, as well as the general scene at the cross that they depict, hark back to Psalm 22:7–8, a poetic messianic prophecy of incredible prescience found in ancient Israel's hymnbook (the book of Psalms): "All they that see me laugh me to scorn: they shoot out the lip, they shake the head, saying, He trusted on the Lord that he would deliver him: let him deliver him, seeing he delighted in him."

To all of these taunts and verbal barbs the Savior answered

nothing. He was the personification of meekness. His goodness showed through his adversity. His character towered over his trauma. Again, we are reminded of Peter's comment: "When he was reviled, [he] reviled not again" (1 Peter 2:23). Even one of the two criminals between whom Jesus was hanging began to goad him. "And one of the malefactors which were hanged railed on him, saying, If thou be Christ, save thyself and us" (Luke 23:39). Still, the Son of God responded to insults with quiet dignity.

Soon, however, the Savior did speak to the second thief because he had rebuked his counterpart for his insolence and also asked for the Savior's mercy. As with the first of the Savior's utterances from the cross (his plea for forgiveness for the soldiers), Luke alone records the Savior's second statement: "But the other answering rebuked him, saying, Dost not thou fear God, seeing thou art in the same condemnation? And we indeed justly; for we receive the due reward of our deeds: but this man hath done nothing amiss. And he said unto Jesus, Lord, remember me when thou comest into thy kingdom. And Jesus said unto him, Verily I say unto thee, To day shalt thou be with me in paradise" (Luke 23:40–43).

Some confusion has arisen through the years regarding the doctrinal implications of Jesus' comment. The crux of the matter seems to lie with the word "paradise," which ultimately derives from a Persian loanword meaning "garden" and could have meant in Jesus' day "the place of the departed." The Prophet Joseph Smith taught that Jesus was saying, "This day thou shalt be with me in the world of spirits" (*Teachings of the Prophet Joseph Smith*, 309). Thus, the fixed principles of repentance were not being altered by Jesus. President Spencer W. Kimball provides powerful doctrinal clarification:

Another mistaken idea is that the thief on the cross was forgiven of his sins when the dying Christ answered: "Today shalt thou be with me in paradise." (Luke 23:43.) These men on the cross were thieves. How could the Lord forgive a malefactor? They had broken laws. There was no doubt of the guilt of the two men, for the one voluntarily confessed their guilt.

The Lord cannot save men *in* their sins but only *from* their sins, and that only when they have shown true repentance. The one thief did show some compassion, whether selfishly with hope we are not sure. He was confessing, but how could he abandon his evil practices when dungeon walls made evil deeds impossible? How could he restore the stolen goods when hanging on the cross? How could he, as John the Baptist required, "bring forth fruits meet for repentance?" How could he live the Lord's commands, attend his meetings, pay his tithing, serve his fellowmen? All these take time. Time was the one thing he was running out of very rapidly. "No unclean thing can enter the kingdom of heaven." This thought has been repeated throughout the scriptures numerous times and is a basic truth. We may be sure that the Savior's instructions to the thief on the cross were comparable to his instructions to the woman caught in adultery: "Go your way and transform yourself and repent."

As the hours passed, the thief's life would ebb out and his spirit would abandon the lifeless body and go into the spirit world, where Christ was going to organize his missionary program. (See 1 Pet. 3:18–20; 4–6.) There he would live along with the antediluvians and all others who had died in their sins. All the Lord's statement promised the thief was that both of them would soon be in the spirit world. The thief's show of repentance on the cross was all to his advantage, but his few words did not nullify a life of sin. The world should know that since the Lord himself cannot save men *in* their sins, no man on earth can administer any sacrament which will do that impossible thing. Hence the mere display of death-bed faith or repentance is not sufficient. (*Miracle of Forgiveness*, 166–67)

Ultimately, we must concede that we do not know the mind of the mercy-seeking thief nor the final disposition of his case. It seems quite possible, however, that he truly was on the road to repentance. We must keep in mind that repentance after this life is a doctrinal reality—else why preach to those spirits in prison who have never heard of Christ nor been converted to him? (1 Peter 3:18–19; 4:6; D&C 138:30–37). Furthermore, we believe that repentance in the spirit world is possible for those of us who knew the truth while in mortality but were not always valiant. We also believe, however, that such repentance is not without additional challenges, as Elder Melvin J. Ballard of the Quorum of the Twelve Apostles declared:

It is my judgment that any man or woman can do more to conform to the laws of God in one year in this life than they could in ten years when they are dead. The spirit only can repent and change, and then the battle has to go forward with the flesh afterwards. It is much easier to overcome and serve the Lord when both flesh and spirit are combined as one. This is the time when men are more pliable and susceptible. When clay is pliable, it is much easier to change than when it gets hard and sets.

This life is the time to repent. That is why I presume it will take a thousand years after the first resurrection until the last group will be prepared to come forth. It will take them a thousand years to do what it would have taken but three score years and ten to accomplish in this life. (Hinckley, *Sermons and Missionary Services of Melvin Joseph Ballard*, 241)

DISCIPLES AT THE CROSS

Just as one would have hoped, not all of the Savior's followers left him alone to face the agonies and humiliations of his crucifixion. Matthew tells us that many women watched the proceedings of the execution from a distance. These women had "followed Jesus from Galilee, ministering unto him" (Matthew 27:55) and were likely among that great company who wept and lamented the Savior's plight as he walked from the place of judgment, the Praetorium, to Golgotha (Luke 23:27). John, writing about the Savior's last moments on the cross, tells us that he, John, was also there with the women at Golgotha, although he never calls himself by name. He refers to himself in his Gospel as the disciple whom Jesus loved (John 13:23; 19:26; 20:2; 21:7, 20).

Close to the end, as his life ebbed away, Jesus looked down from the cross and, seeing his mother as well as the disciple whom he loved, made his third utterance: "Woman, behold thy son! Then saith he to the disciple, Behold thy mother! And from that hour that disciple took her unto his own home" (John 19:26–27).

Though "Woman," the form of address used by Jesus to

speak to his mother, may sound harsh to modern ears, it was, in the culture of that day, a term of endearment and respect. Jesus seems to be saying something like, "Dear Woman, you see the circumstances your Son is in. I won't be around much longer, but John will care for you as though you were his own mother."

No doubt a special bond existed between the Savior and John the Beloved, but that does not diminish Jesus' love for the other disciples. He cared for each one individually. Jesus may have singled out John to care for His mother because John had the desire and the means to do so and because he was there at Golgotha with his own mother. John's mother, who would have heard her son's special commission from the Savior, would also have been able to help care for Mary. Matthew's Gospel mentions the mother of the sons of Zebedee (of whom John was one) being in attendance at the cross (Matthew 27:56), and Mark apparently gives her name: Salome (Matthew 4:21; Mark 15:40).

It is also possible that John's relationship with the Savior was familial—that is, John the Beloved may have been a cousin of Jesus. Both Matthew and Mark name three women at Golgotha: Mary Magdalene; Mary, the mother of James (the Less) and Joses; and the mother of Zebedee's sons, or Salome. John appears to name four women: Mary Magdalene; Mary, the mother of Jesus; "his mother's sister"; and Mary, the wife of Cleophas (John 19:25). Could Salome, the mother of Zebedee's sons, be the same person as the sister of Mary, the mother of Jesus? Though we cannot know with certainty, other students of the New Testament have considered it. Elder James E. Talmage wrote: "From the fact that John mentions the mother of Jesus and 'his mother's sister' (19:25) and omits mention of Salome by name, some expositors hold that Salome was the sister of Mary the mother of Jesus; and therefore the Savior's aunt. This relationship would makes James and John cousins to Jesus" (*Jesus the Christ*, 521).

It makes perfect sense that John the Beloved would possess a special relationship with Jesus, being his "beloved disciple" on the basis of family connection and not on the basis of arbitrary favoritism. Also, Jesus' saying to John, "Behold thy mother," reflects a genuine family relationship, and John is being asked to care for his aunt, his "other mother," as she would have been regarded in that culture. Furthermore, it seems likely that although many women would have been near the crucifixion site, Jesus would have specifically spoken to members of his biological family—his mother, cousin, and aunt—as he neared the end of his life. The early Church of Jesus Christ was a family affair in many ways. John the Baptist was a cousin of the Savior, and the original Quorum of the Twelve included at least two sets of brothers and probably three: Peter and Andrew (John 1:40), James and John (Matthew 4:21), and probably Matthew and James, who was nicknamed the Less to distinguish him from James the son of Zebedee (Mark 2:14; Matthew 10:3). That the mother of James the Less was also waiting by the cross may hint at a strong relationship between her and Mary, the mother of Jesus.

THE CHARACTER OF CHRIST

The few recorded statements made by the Savior on the cross teach us much about him. "It might well be stated as a rule of human nature that when a man reaches his greatest extremity, a moment of extreme danger, pain, emotion, or critical need, a point in life which is marked by imminent destruction or death, the true nature of his soul becomes evident." Is he basically thoughtful or selfish, courageous or cowardly, self-absorbed or concerned with others? During the most trying and difficult circumstances of life, an individual's "words mirror his innermost soul. His speech betrays what his character is really like—the quality of his concerns, his compassion, his love—the whole focus or thrust of his life, whether noble or mean, depraved or exalted" (*Life and Teachings of Jesus and His Apostles*, 185).

The greatest example of this principle is found in Jesus of Nazareth. While he hung and suffered on the cross, his petition for forgiveness on behalf of the Roman soldiers who carried out the order of execution demonstrates his basic nature. His mercy and compassion, which constitute the very essence of who and what he is, were demonstrated many times during his life—to the leper (Mark 1:41), to the man possessed (Mark 5:19), to the whole multitude during a moment of personal sadness (Matthew 14:14), and on, and on, and on. His acts of forgiveness grow out of his pure love, or perfect charity (Moroni 7:47).

The Savior's mercy, compassion, forgiveness, and pure love will be extended to all, even at the time of judgment. President J. Reuben Clark Jr. said: "I feel that [the Lord] will give that punishment which is the very least that our transgression will justify. . . . I believe that when it comes to making the rewards for our good conduct, he will give the maximum that is possible to give" (*As Ye Sow*, 7–8).

It is likewise apparent from President Clark's comments that mercy does not rob justice. Jesus was loving, kind, fair, and compassionate. But he was not indulgent. Elder McConkie wrote that on the cross "Jesus did not, it should be noted, pray for Judas who betrayed him; for Caiaphas and the chief priests who conspired against him; for the false witnesses who perjured their souls before the Sanhedrin and in the judgment halls of Rome; for Pilate and Herod, either of whom could have freed him; nor for Lucifer whose power and persuasive ability underlay the whole wicked procedure. All these are left in the hands of Eternal Justice to be dealt with according to their works. Mercy cannot rob justice; the guilty do not go free simply because the righteous bring no railing accusation against them" (*Doctrinal New Testament Commentary*, 1:819).

The Savior thought of others to the very end of his life. To the mercy-seeking thief on the cross, Jesus extended a merciful response. To his mother, Jesus demonstrated love and concern for her welfare in the midst of his own terrible suffering. He knew what his mother was going through as she saw the unspeakable horrors of crucifixion snuffing out the life of her precious Son. She was now witnessing the fulfillment of a prophecy made thirty-three years before in the Temple in Jerusalem when she had officially presented her infant Son to the righteous witnesses in the house of the Lord. At that time Simeon foretold the future to Mary, as Luke records: "And Simeon blessed them, and said unto Mary his mother, Behold, this child is set for the fall and rising again of many in Israel; and for a sign which shall be spoken against; (Yea, a sword shall pierce through thy own soul also,) that the thoughts of many hearts may be revealed" (Luke 2:34–35).

Now, thirty-three years later, Mary was witnessing the death throes of her Son on the cross and experiencing the fulfillment of Simeon's prophecy. As Simeon indicated, Mary would be pierced emotionally when her Son was pierced physically. Jesus knew of this circumstance, and of course he wanted to ease his mother's pain. Therefore, "with supreme solicitude, and though he himself was in agony on the cross, Jesus [placed] his mother in the care and keeping of John" (McConkie, *Doctrinal New Testament Commentary*, 1:826).

The Savior was continually, inevitably, thinking of the welfare of others to the very end. From his comments on the cross we learn of the essence of the Savior's personality: his merciful and forgiving nature, his concern for others, his endurance in patience, and his character and supreme goodness. How grateful we should be that we can call him our Master.

Now from the sixth hour there was darkness over all the land unto the ninth hour.

And about the ninth hour Jesus cried with a loud voice, saying, Eli, Eli, lama sabachthani? that is to say, My God, my God, why hast thou forsaken me?

Some of them that stood there, when they heard that, said, This man calleth for Elias.

MATTHEW 27:45–47

CHAPTER 10

Darkness and Abandonment

T he Synoptic Gospels all report that about the sixth hour of the day (noon), darkness gathered over the whole land and remained until the ninth hour, or 3 P.M. (Matthew 27:45; Mark 15:33; Luke 23:44). We can imagine that as the life of the Savior waned under the horrible effects of crucifixion, the darkness in the world grew thicker. Just as it was light for a day and a night and a day when Jesus, the Light of the World, came into the world (3 Nephi 1:15), so now nature was beginning to dim, preparing to reel and convulse, as the death of Jesus approached and the Light of the World would make his exit from the world. All this was in accord with prophecy uttered years before by Samuel the Lamanite (Helaman 14:20).

Certainly, there is much we do not know about the physics of the universe and much to be explored regarding the physical connection between the Lord of Light and the light we discern every day. Yet, the crucifixion helps us to see that the Prophet Joseph Smith's cosmological revelation on the nature of light, life, and our Redeemer is far more than just metaphor. That single revelation tells us why darkness gathered on the earth from the sixth to the ninth hour, until the sun itself was eclipsed (the Greek word in Luke 23:45 is *eklipontos*).

> This is the light of Christ. As also he is in the sun, and the light of the sun, and the power thereof by which it was made.
>
> As also he is in the moon, and is the light of the moon, and the power thereof by which it was made;
>
> As also the light of the stars, and the power thereof by which they were made;
>
> And the earth also, and the power thereof, even the earth upon which you stand.
>
> Which light proceedeth forth from the presence of God to fill the immensity of space—
>
> The light which is in all things, which giveth life to all things, which is the law by which all things are governed, even the power of God who sitteth upon his throne, who is in the bosom of eternity, who is in the midst of all things. (D&C 88:7–10, 12–13)

THE SAVIOR ABANDONED BY HIS FATHER: PROPHECY FULFILLED

As the ninth hour arrived, according to Matthew and Mark, Jesus cried out with a loud and startling (as the text implies) voice. It must have been a great surprise to those who were not expecting such volume from one so weakened from the tortures he had endured and who appeared to be teetering on the brink of death. "*Eli, Eli, lama sabachthani?*" "My God, my God, why hast thou forsaken me?" (Matthew 27:46; Mark 15:34). The Aramaic verb here, *shabaq,* means to "leave alone," "to abandon." This fourth statement from the cross is a direct quotation, uttered in Aramaic, from the opening verse of Psalm 22, that unparalleled poetic prophecy of the Atonement. This profoundly agonized query from the Savior was a fulfillment of the inspired prediction by Israel's psalmist almost a thousand years before and which had been chanted by Israel for centuries as one of their hymns.

We cannot fully appreciate nor comprehend the terror and spiritual pain so great as to produce in that moment so anguished a cry from God himself. Perhaps only those who have experienced the torment of real abandonment, the abject misery of true loneliness, can begin to appreciate the feelings the Savior was enduring. Personally, I can only begin to relate to his feelings when I contemplate my emotions at three different times in my life: the panic I felt as a child the first time I was lost in a huge crowd far from home; the horrors my mind conjured up when I was unable to find one of my own small children in a potentially dangerous situation; and the profound sense of loss I experienced when my father died. I was a young teenager and those were difficult days—a time of great aloneness. But I suspect that these three episodes do not begin to approach the Savior's experience.

President Brigham Young taught that Jesus was left completely alone by his Father once before—in the Garden of Gethsemane—and that experience was so traumatic, so devastating, so utterly horrible for the sinless Son of God that it alone caused him to sweat blood. Said President Young, "If he [Jesus] had had the power of God upon him, he would not have sweat blood; but all was withdrawn from him, and a veil was cast over him" (*Journal of Discourses*, 3:206). I take "all" to mean "everything."

Now, upon the cross of Golgotha, the horror he knew in Gethsemane returned. These were the only two times in his life when he was truly alone. Friends and family could abandon him, and he could take that kind of forsakenness. The one thing he could not take, the one thing far worse for him than everything else, was abandonment by his Father, the total loss of his Father's sustaining influence. To this one Being who was perfect, without sin, who had always enjoyed his Father's closeness and unrestrained Spirit, abandonment by his Father was more than he could bear. Because Jesus was perfect, he was perfectly sensitized to the Spirit. He possessed the Spirit in its fulness, whereas each of us possesses only a measure of it and to a greater or lesser degree (JST John 3:34). Total absence of his Father's influence was spiritual death, the very atmosphere of hell itself, the deepest pit of despair, the darkest depression. To go from possessing the fulness of the Father's Spirit to having it completely withdrawn, totally absent, produced in Jesus an intensity of agony such as no other being will experience or endure. He descended below *all* things (D&C 88:6; 122:8).

We might be tempted to argue that others, including sons of perdition, have known or will know this kind of hell, but that would not be true. No one started out from the same point as the Savior did, and thus no one ever has or ever will go as low—no one! Even for the Savior, greater pain or anguish was not possible. One simply cannot go lower than below *all* things.

LESSONS FOR HIS DISCIPLES

All of this discussion of the extremity that the Savior had to endure is not to discount the pain or the loneliness or the anguish of abandonment that the rest of Heavenly Father's children experience in their mortal lives. Rather, it serves to emphasize, in a monumental way, three uplifting and comforting truths.

First, Jesus can succor us and nurture us precisely because he has perfect empathy. To provide succor implies something more than nurturing. It connotes someone running to another to provide aid or help. It aptly depicts the Savior's inherent essence and personality. That is the reason that he, being God, came to earth as a mortal.

> And he shall go forth, suffering pains and afflictions and temptations of every kind; and this that the word might be fulfilled which saith he will take upon him the pains and the sicknesses of his people.
>
> And he will take upon him death, that he may loose the bands of death which bind his people; and he will take upon him their infirmities, that his bowels may be filled with mercy, according to the flesh, that *he may know according to the flesh how to succor his people* according to their infirmities. (Alma 7:11–12; emphasis added)

Notice the phrase "according to the flesh." Jesus knows from his own mortal experience *what* to do to assist us and *how* best to do it. "For in that he himself hath suffered being tempted, he is able to succor them that are tempted"—or sick, or in pain, or lonely or abandoned, or afflicted with a thousand other maladies or challenges or handicaps (Hebrews 2:18). President John Taylor testified:

> It was necessary, when the Savior was upon the earth, that he should be tempted in all points, like unto us, and "be touched with the feeling of our infirmities," [Hebrews 4:15] to comprehend the weaknesses and

strength, the perfections and imperfections of poor fallen human nature. And having accomplished the thing he came into the world to do: having had to grapple with the hypocrisy, corruption, weakness, and imbecility of man; having met with temptation and trial in all its various forms, and overcome; he has become a "faithful high priest" [Hebrews 2:17] to intercede for us in the everlasting kingdom of his Father.

He knows how to estimate and put a proper value upon human nature, for he, having been placed in the same position as we are, knows how to bear with our weaknesses and infirmities, and can fully comprehend the depth, power, and strength of the afflictions and trials that men have to cope with in this world. And thus understandingly and by experience, he can bear with them. (*John Taylor*, 53)

Jesus is perfectly sensitized to each of our trials, our circumstances of loneliness, because he alone experienced all of them—absorbed to himself our pain and abject misery. The bad things in life cannot magically be made to disappear, but Jesus can help us through them, can take the burdens that come from them, until they trouble us no more.

Second, as a result of the Savior's anguished cry at Golgotha, we come to understand that no one in mortality is exempt from suffering of the highest order, not even God. We also better understand *why* we are going through tough times—especially tough times all alone. It is all part of the grand design to help us grow, as Elder Neal A. Maxwell taught:

There is, in the suffering of the highest order, a point that is reached—a point of aloneness—when the individual (as did the Savior on a much grander scale) must bear it, as it were, alone. Even the faithful may wonder if they can take any more or if they are in some way forsaken.

Those who, as it were, stand on the foot of the cross often can do so little to help absorb the pain and the anguish. It is something we must bear ourselves in order that our triumph can be complete. Elder James E. Talmage said of the Savior at the point of greatest suffering on the cross, "that the supreme sacrifice of the Son might be consummated in all its fulness, the Father seems to have withdrawn the support of His immediate Presence, leaving to the Savior of men the glory of complete victory over the forces of sin and death." (*Jesus the Christ*, p. 661.)

Thus there ought to be expectations that in this laboratory of life we will actually see each other in the process of being remodeled, sometimes succeeding and sometimes failing. We will obviously be aware of others who are also in the "furnace of affliction." However, we will not always have a smooth, ready answer to the question, "Why me?" "Why now?" "Why this?"—for as Moroni observed, "Ye receive no witness until *after* the trial of your faith." (Ether 12:6. Italics added.) (*All These Things Shall Give Thee Experience*, 43–44)

Third, a reciprocal truth operates. Because Jesus' disciples will pass through something of his experiences, including loneliness and abandonment in its many forms, we are privileged to understand to a degree what he went through and cultivate empathy for him—even coming to know what he knows and receiving what he has received as a result of our own faithful suffering and trials. "If we suffer, we shall also reign with him: if we deny him, he also will deny us" (2 Timothy 2:12).

Faithful endurance and loyalty to God in the face of feeling abandoned, feeling loneliness of every kind, is one of the key ways God has of sifting and sorting as well as of teaching. God's prophets, too, have been tried in the furnace of abandonment. Elijah, the powerful guardian of priesthood keys, at one point complained to the Lord because he felt abandoned to carry the weight of the world on his shoulders: "And he said, I have been very jealous for the Lord God of hosts: because the children of Israel have forsaken thy covenant, thrown down thine altars, and slain thy prophets with the sword; and I, even I only, am left; and they seek my life, to take it away" (1 Kings 19:14). Ultimately, the Lord helped Elijah to see that he was not alone and that all things supported divine purposes. Because of Elijah's faithfulness in the face of life-threatening circumstances, he was blessed and taken into heaven (2 Kings 2:11).

On the other hand, there have been prophets and others whose lives did not have a happy ending in mortality even though they remained faithful and true during long periods of feeling abandoned. Perhaps the most notable and heart-wrenching example is that of the Prophet Joseph Smith. We cannot read the opening lines to Doctrine and Covenants 121 without noticing the obvious parallels to the Savior's experience at Golgotha. "O God, where art thou? And where is the pavil-ion that covereth thy hiding place?" (D&C 121:1). Perhaps Joseph's cry, like the Savior's, is the elemental expression of all those who, at some point, have experienced tragedy or feelings of unrelenting loneliness or feelings of abandonment. And like Joseph, we will come to know we have not, nor ever will be, abandoned like the Savior was. We may ask for, and receive, assurances of our Father's watchful care. The act of asking is important. And if we are patient, we will see just how much both Jesus and Joseph can teach us about the hows and whys of pain, sorrow, suffering, and tribulations.

My son, peace be unto thy soul; thine adversity and thine afflictions shall be but a small moment;

And then, if thou endure it well, God shall exalt thee on high; thou shalt triumph over all thy foes. (D&C 121:7–8)

If thou art called to pass through tribulation; if thou art in perils among false brethren; if thou art in perils among robbers; if thou art in perils by land or by sea. . . .

And if thou shouldst be cast into the pit, or into the hands of murderers, and the sentence of death passed upon thee; if thou be cast into the deep; if the billowing surge conspire against thee; if fierce winds become thine enemy; if the heavens gather blackness, and all the elements combine to hedge up the way; and above all, if the very jaws of hell shall gape open the mouth wide after thee, know thou, my son, that all these things shall give thee experience, and shall be for thy good.

The Son of Man hath descended below them all. Art thou greater than he? (D&C 122:5, 7–8)

Joseph Smith remained faithful and had his exaltation sealed upon him (D&C 132:49). But we also note that Joseph's life did not turn out as Elijah's did, nor did it end up the way Joseph may have thought it would at the time he was sealed up, owing to the unusual wording of the last part of God's promise to him: "I have seen your sacrifices in obedience to that which I have told you. Go, therefore, and I make a way for your escape, as I accepted the offering of Abraham of his son Isaac" (D&C 132:50). Abraham, of course, was not required to offer up the life of Isaac. God made a way for Isaac's escape by providing a ram in the thicket (Genesis 22:12–13). In the end, however, there was no ram in the thicket for Joseph Smith, and he was required to give his life.

The point here is that God's ways are different from man's ways. He "seeth not as man seeth" (1 Samuel 16:7). He regards a happy ending in eternity of infinitely greater worth than a so-called happy ending in mortality, especially considering the way some men and women understand happiness. We have been promised by the Lord that he will make a way for our escape in our lives (1 Corinthians 10:13). But we must remember that our ways are not God's ways, and sometimes life's episodes do not conform to storybook endings. Mortal life is not fair. The lives of both Jesus Christ and Joseph Smith demonstrate that. But because of the life and death of Jesus Christ, because of his willing submissiveness in the face of total abandonment on the cross, he has the right, and the power, and the unwavering desire to make up to us all of the unfairness of life. Even though we may not be able to understand why things happen the way they do (and it is usually pointless to think about that question very much), we know that our Heavenly Father and Jesus Christ love us perfectly. And we know with perfect surety that we will be compensated for every trial, tragedy, and sorrow, every episode of loneliness, abandonment, and undeserved suffering. Christian theologian Richard Mouw said it well:

> We admit that we can't understand the mysteries of God's purposes. But we can go to the cross of Jesus

Christ. We can see that, at the cross, God took upon himself that abandonment, that abuse, that forlornness, that depth of suffering, Christ himself cried out from the depths of his being, 'My God, why hast thou forsaken me?' When we see what God did, through Jesus Christ, we can say, 'Yes, there is a safe place in the universe, in the shelter of the Almighty, in the shadow of the Most High.' That place we know to be *Calvary*. ("Christian Responses to a World in Crisis," 11).

What was said long ago by chief apostle Peter bears repeating. Fiery trials work a great work in us. They are more precious than gold, for if faithfully endured, they bring us eternal glory (1 Peter 1:7). One of the truly great doctrines is this: Adversity and suffering make the veil very thin. President Harold B. Lee indicated that because of his struggles and trials the veil had become thin and that perhaps the veil would even have disappeared had the trials been greater:

"I thank the Lord that I may have passed some of the tests, but maybe there will have to be more before I shall have been polished to do all that the Lord would have me do.

"Sometimes when the veil has been very thin, I have thought that if the struggle had been still greater that maybe then there would have been no veil. I stand by, not asking for anything more than the Lord wants to give me, but I know that he is up there and he is guiding and directing" (Conference Report, October 1973, 170).

What Isaiah said more than twenty-seven hundred years ago ought to have great meaning to us today: "But now, O Lord, thou art our father; we are the clay, and thou our potter; and we all are the work of thy hand" (Isaiah 64:8). Raw clay usually

155

does not possess immediate beauty or usefulness. Similarly, most of us human beings, if not all, are not the best, most valuable vessels we can be without significant shaping. But if we allow the Master Potter, the Lord, to put his hand to our lives and mold us, he can and will make us into enduring vessels of beauty and strength. The tools he uses to do the shaping are those kind of painful moments the Savior himself experienced in his mortal life, right up to the end.

Make no mistake about it. Our Heavenly Father and his divine Son are not interested in merely saving us. They want to change us, reshape us, transform us. In truth, full and complete salvation, what we know to be exaltation, cannot occur unless we are transformed. But the reshaping, the changing, and the transforming are painful. A parable from the writer George MacDonald, made famous by English churchman and theologian C. S. Lewis, is wonderfully illustrative:

> Imagine yourself as a living house. God comes in to rebuild that house. At first, perhaps, you can understand what He is doing. He is getting the drains right and stopping the leaks in the roof and so on: you knew that those jobs needed doing and so you are not surprised. But presently he starts knocking the house about in a way that hurts abominably and does not seem to make sense. What on earth is He up to? The explanation is that He is building quite a different house from the one you thought of—throwing out a new wing here, putting on an extra floor there, running up towers, making courtyards. You thought you were going to be made into a decent little cottage: but He is building a palace. He

intends to come and live in it Himself. (*Mere Christianity*, 176)

The tools God uses to shape and transform us are trials, tribulations, and suffering. Suffering of the highest order—the kind that comes not as a natural result of mortality or our own transgressions but as a result of what God himself gives to us—is customized to our spiritual needs. Our trials are tailor-made for each one of us, uniquely crafted for our individual circumstances and personalities. But I have noticed that often in these customized trials and suffering there is a common element: the feeling at some point of somehow being abandoned or betrayed or left alone by God at a time when he is desperately needed.

C. S. Lewis indicates that he experienced this feeling of abandonment when, after years of writing and speaking about God's personal interest in our suffering, he had to endure the pain and sorrow of losing his wife, Joy, to cancer. That was the greatest trial of his life. He felt that God had left him on his own to flounder, that God was not attuning His ear, that the portals of heaven were shut tight and locked. Lewis records his initial feelings in the face of his great trial: "Where is God? . . . Go to Him when your need is desperate, when all other help is vain, and what do you find? A door slammed in your face, and a sound of bolting and double bolting on the inside. After that, silence" (*Grief Observed*, 21–22).

Lewis is honest enough to let us see that he asked the same questions other noble and great disciples have asked: "Where are you, God? Why are you abandoning me?" It seems to me that such an experience is very much like the Savior's own experience at Golgotha. Jesus did not doubt the existence of his Father. He knew he was there. It was just that he felt his Father had left him alone at his time of greatest need. The lesson we learn is that all of us are given a glimpse, a taste, of Jesus' very experience during the Atonement: "My God, my God, why hast thou forsaken me?" (Matthew 27:46).

Lewis observes that God does not abandon us but allows us to learn crucial lessons we can learn *only* by experience, and He monitors our growth. Lewis gives us a window of insight into his own growth when he recorded: "I have gradually been coming to feel that the door is no longer shut and bolted. Was it my own frantic need that slammed it in my face? The time when there is nothing at all in your soul except a cry for help may be just the time when God can't give it: you are like the drowning man who can't be helped because he clutches and grabs. Perhaps your own reiterated cries deafen you to the voice you hoped to hear.

"On the other hand, 'Knock and it shall be opened.' But does knocking mean hammering and kicking the door like a maniac?" (*Grief Observed*, 63–64).

Elder Neal A. Maxwell, a man well acquainted with C. S. Lewis and a man whose own trials have qualified him to teach with authenticity, has said:

> To those of you who so suffer and who, neverthe-less, so endure and so testify by the eloquence of your examples, we salute you in Christ! Please forgive those of us who clumsily try to comfort you. We know from whence your true comfort comes. God's 'bosom' is there to be leaned upon. . . .
>
> We can confidently cast our cares upon the Lord because, through the agonizing events of Gethsemane and Calvary, atoning Jesus is already familiar with our

sins, sicknesses, and sorrows (see 1 Pet. 5:7; 2 Ne. 9:21; Alma 7:11–12). He can carry them now because He has successfully carried them before (see 2 Ne. 9:8). ("Yet Thou Art There," 32–33).

The scriptures teach us that God has not forsaken us nor will he ever forsake us. He is waiting and able to help us in our extremity. No less powerful to help is his divine Son, who has perfect empathy for us and can carry us through those times when we cannot go on, precisely because of his own experience. In fact, one reason Jesus was abandoned by his Father in Gethsemane and on the cross of Golgotha was so he could descend below all things to know every human circumstance and thus emerge victor over all things, with the knowledge and power to help us. By his confirming witness, I know that Jesus suffered on the cross the fierceness of the wrath of Almighty God, and because Jesus suffered that wrath on the cross, I do not have to. Even more important, I know that because Jesus was lifted up on the cross, I can be lifted up also—to eternal life. Furthermore, I know that because God forsook his Son on the cross, he will never have to forsake me.

And straightway one of them ran, and took a spunge, and filled it with vinegar, and put it on a reed, and gave him to drink.

The rest said, Let be, let us see whether Elias will come to save him.

Jesus, when he had cried again with a loud voice, yielded up the ghost.

And, behold, the veil of the temple was rent in twain from the top to the bottom; and the earth did quake, and the rocks rent.

Now when the centurion, and they that were with him, watching Jesus, saw the earthquake, and those things that were done, they feared greatly, saying, Truly this was the Son of God.

When the even was come, there came a rich man of Arimathaea, named Joseph, who also himself was Jesus' disciple:

He went to Pilate, and begged the body of Jesus. . . . And when Joseph had taken the body, he wrapped it in a clean linen cloth,

And laid it in his own new tomb, which he had hewn out in the rock: and he rolled a great stone to the door of the sepulchre, and departed.

And there was Mary Magdalene, and the other Mary, sitting over against the sepulchre.

MATTHEW 27:48–51, 54, 57–61

And there came also Nicodemus, which at the first came to Jesus by night, and brought a mixture of myrrh and aloes, about an hundred pound weight. Then took they the body of Jesus, and wound it in linen clothes with the spices, as the manner of the Jews is to bury.

Now in the place where he was crucified there was a garden; and in the garden a new sepulchre, wherein was never man yet laid.

There laid they Jesus therefore because of the Jews' preparation day; for the sepulchre was nigh at hand.

JOHN 19:39–42

CHAPTER 11

Death and Burial

The Savior's tortured cry of abandonment that awful Friday afternoon was misunderstood by some of the crowd gathered at the cross. They apparently thought it was a plea for help from the ancient prophet Elijah. Perhaps this misunderstanding was influenced by a Jewish tradition that Elijah often came to the aid of those in distress. But Jesus received no help, no angelic intervention, as he had in Gethsemane. He had to face the terrible consequences of Golgotha alone in order to come off conqueror over death and hell and to satisfy the demands of justice. "In that bitterest hour the dying Christ was alone, alone in most terrible reality. That the supreme sacrifice of the Son might be consummated in all its fulness, the Father seems to have withdrawn the support of His immediate Presence, leaving to the Savior of men *the glory of complete victory* over the forces of sin and death" (Talmage, *Jesus the Christ*, 661).

THE END APPROACHES: PROPHECY FULFILLED

After Jesus had endured hours of unlimited pain and partial asphyxiation, the pericardium (the sack around the heart)

161

would have begun to fill up with serum and compress the heart. As Jesus tried to move his body up and down to facilitate breathing, his already lacerated back would have been torn open again by the rough wood of the cross. His lungs would have made a frantic effort to gulp even small amounts of air. Loss of body fluid would have created heavy, thick, sluggish blood and made it increasingly difficult for the heart to pump. Dehydration would have been at a critical level (Davis, "Physician Testifies about Crucifixion," 39). At this point, Jesus uttered his fifth statement from the cross: "I thirst" (John 19:28). Here, the poetic prophecy of Psalm 22 is again recalled: "My strength is dried up like a potsherd; and my tongue cleaveth to my jaws; and thou hast brought me into the dust of death" (v. 15).

Because the Romans knew what developments to expect from their crucified victims, a small vessel of vinegar had been set near the cross of Jesus, and one of the crowd ran and "filled a spunge with vinegar, and put it upon hyssop, and put it to [Jesus'] mouth" (John 19:29). This action fulfilled another of the poetic messianic prophecies of the Psalmist: "And in my thirst they gave me vinegar to drink" (Psalm 69:21). But the event also harked back to the inauguration of the ancient Passover ordinance when the use of hyssop was instituted as a type or symbol of the atoning sacrifice of Jesus Christ: "Then Moses called for all the elders of Israel, and said unto them, Draw out and take you a lamb according to your families, and kill the passover. And ye shall take a bunch of hyssop, and dip it in the blood that is in the bason, and strike the lintel and the two side posts with the blood that is in the bason; and none of you shall go out at the door of his house until the morning" (Exodus 12:21–22). Again, we are made to appreciate the principle taught by ancient prophets: "All things which have been given of God from the beginning of the world, unto man, are the typifying of him" (2 Nephi 11:4).

Once all things had been accomplished that were intended by God and comprehended in his sweeping plan of salvation, Jesus cried out in a loud voice, bowed his head, and gave up the ghost. "Sweet and welcome as would have been the relief of death in any of the earlier stages of His suffering from Gethsemane to the cross, He lived until all things were accomplished as had been appointed" (Talmage, *Jesus the Christ*, 662). John 19:30 records: "When Jesus therefore had received the vinegar, he said, It is finished: and he bowed his head, and gave up the ghost."

Joseph Smith's translation of Matthew 27:54, provided in the LDS edition of the Bible (footnote 50a), gives us the full account of the Savior's sixth statement from the cross: "Jesus, when he had cried again with a loud voice, saying, Father it is finished, *thy will is done*" (emphasis added). This utterance is tremendously significant. It encapsulates the whole plan of salvation; it sums up the whole reason Jesus was sent to earth: to do his Father's will, as he himself had indicated on other occasions (John 6:38; 3 Nephi 27:13–14). The Prophet's translation of Matthew 27:54 brings us full circle to the time in premortality when the Savior volunteered to be our Redeemer, to do the will of the Father, and to let all the honor be his—"Father, thy will be done, and the glory be thine forever" (Moses 4:2).

The will of the Son was fully swallowed up in the will of the Father. The unparalleled prayer and desire of the Savior articulated in Gethsemane—"thy will be done"—was now fulfilled in every way, completely satisfying every aim, goal, purpose, and requirement of the plan of salvation. That is, in actuality, the sense of the Greek verb used in John's account of Jesus' sixth statement: "It is *finished*" (John 19:30; emphasis added). The verb translated into English as "finished" is *tetelestai* (from *teleo*), which means "to fulfill something, to make something complete." That is what Golgotha did. That which was started in Gethsemane was completed at Golgotha. How grateful we ought to be for the Prophet Joseph Smith's illuminating efforts to help us appreciate more completely the Savior's work and words.

Immediately after making this significant sixth declaration, Jesus uttered his final statement in mortality, as only Luke tells us: "Father, into thy hands I commend my spirit: and having said thus, he gave up the ghost" (Luke 23:46).

THE MORTAL DEATH OF GOD

The very Son of God had died. The God who created the universe had experienced mortal death and passed through the veil to the spirit world, just as each of us will do. His physical body ceased to function. He now knew from his own experience what death was like—and the most horrible, torturous form of death that can be imagined. It should not be thought, however, that his decease was due merely to the natural processes of organ failure. Jesus died because he voluntarily gave up his life. Perhaps it might be said that the enervating effects of crucifixion brought him to the point where he could choose to give up his mortal life. But it was ultimately his choice—the only Being we know of with the power to determine the moment of his own decease. Death did not have power over him, did not control him. He controlled it. He decided to submit to it.

The Savior taught this doctrine when he said, "For as the Father hath life in himself; so hath he given to the Son to have life in himself" (John 5:26). "Therefore doth my Father love me, because I lay down my life, that I might take it again. No man taketh it from me, but I lay it down of myself. I have power to lay it down, and I have power to take it again. This commandment have I received of my Father" (John 10:17–18). In other words, our Father in Heaven passed on genetically to his literal, biological Son the power of life. That is why it is so crucial to possess a correct understanding of Jesus' literal, divine Sonship. The nature of his birth determined the nature of his death. Thus, possessing the genetic makeup of his Father—life—Jesus had power over death, could determine the time of his death, and have the power to take up his mortal body again, which he would do after three days.

Jesus possessed the powers and attributes of eternal life independently, "on the same principle that His Father who gave Him these divine powers and attributes possesses them," and this gave Jesus the ability to choose to die only after all things necessary to the plan had been accomplished (Andrus, *God, Man, and the Universe*, 417). But another factor also influenced the Savior's death: the withdrawal of the Father's Spirit and power. The Father's Spirit is pure life and light, especially the intensity or extent to which Jesus enjoyed it. As the Joseph Smith Translation says in John 3:34, "For God giveth him [Jesus] not the Spirit by measure, *for he dwelleth in him, even the fulness*" (emphasis added). In short, Jesus was able to die because the Father completely withdrew his life-giving, life-sustaining influence and powers.

Thus, here is another reason for the Father's withdrawal from his Son. Besides the need for the Son to descend below all things, besides the requirement that Jesus suffer spiritual death and hell, besides the need for him to know all our circumstances in order to be able to succor us according to the flesh, the Father withdrew from Jesus so that he, the Son, could have the sole power to determine his own death. "The Savior of the world was left alone by His Father to experience, of His own free will and choice, an act of agency which allowed Him to complete His mission of the Atonement" (Hales, "Behold, We Count Them Happy Which Endure," 75).

If the Father had not withdrawn from the Son again on the cross as he did in Gethsemane, Jesus would have been sustained and nourished by the life and light of his Father's Spirit. Total degeneration of the body could not have occurred, and thus he could not have died by an act of will so readily. One gospel scholar has approached the idea from a slightly different angle but with the same basic principle in mind: "The withdrawal of the Spirit from Jesus, with the influence which the powers of spiritual death and darkness then had upon Him, apparently caused a critical breakdown to occur in His bodily organs and tissues so that, when He willed that He should die, His spirit could readily depart into the spirit world" (Andrus, *God, Man, and the Universe*, 425).

THE TESTIMONY OF NATURE: PROPHECY FULFILLED

At the moment Jesus died, the Synoptic Gospels record, "the veil of the temple was rent in twain from the top to the bottom" (Matthew 27:51; Mark 15:38; Luke 23:45). Matthew adds, "And the earth did quake, and the rocks rent." It is to be expected that all nature would convulse and the earth would mourn while darkness covered the land because the Light and Life of the World had departed the world. As Nephi had said six hundred years earlier, "The rocks of the earth must rend" because "the God of nature suffers" (1 Nephi 19:12). This earthquake was also a graphic fulfillment of the ancient prophecy given by Enoch when he had his vision of the crucifixion. "And the Lord said unto Enoch: Look, and he looked and beheld the Son of Man lifted up on the cross, after the manner of men; and he heard a loud voice; and the heavens were veiled; and all the creations of God mourned; and the earth groaned; and the rocks were rent" (Moses 7:55–56).

This upheaval in the Holy Land paralleled events occurring on the American continent at the death of the Savior. The geologic destruction had been prophesied by Samuel the Lamanite more than thirty years before:

> Yea, at the time that he shall yield up the ghost there shall be thunderings and lightnings for the space of many hours, and the earth shall shake and tremble; and the rocks which are upon the face of this earth, which are both above the earth and beneath, which ye know at this time are solid, or the more part of it is one solid mass, shall be broken up;

> Yea, they shall be rent in twain, and shall ever after be found in seams and in cracks, and in broken fragments upon the face of the whole earth, yea, both above the earth and beneath.

> And behold, there shall be great tempests, and there shall be many mountains laid low, like unto a valley, and there shall be many places which are now called valleys which shall become mountains, whose height is great.

> And many highways shall be broken up, and many cities shall become desolate. (Helaman 14:21–24)

TESTIMONY OF THE TEMPLE VEIL

Even more startling and horrifying, at least to the Jewish leaders, was that at the time of the Savior's death the veil of the Temple, the great curtain that had separated the Holy Place from the Most Holy Place, or Holy of Holies, was torn asunder. The most sacred room in the Temple was now exposed. The priests and Jewish leaders would have looked upon this scene with horror. The holiest place on earth was desecrated. God's sanctity was violated. Such a devastating occurrence symbolized the end of the Mosaic dispensation, the fulfillment of the law of Moses, and the opening of a new dispensation with the restoration of the higher law and the greater availability of the Melchizedek Priesthood. It was a dramatic announcement of the fulness of the Gospel as the new and only acceptable covenant. It was also a signal sent by God himself, as Elder McConkie described:

> The veil itself . . . is said to have been sixty feet long, thirty feet wide, "of the thickness of the palm of the hand, and wrought in 72 squares, which were joined together." It was so heavy that it took hundreds of priests to manipulate it. "If the Veil was at all such as is described in the Talmud, it could not have been rent in twain by a mere earthquake or the fall of the lintel, although its composition in squares fastened together might explain, how the rent might be as described in the Gospel.
>
> Indeed, everything seems to indicate that, although the earthquake might furnish the physical basis, the rent of the Temple-Veil was—with reverence be it said— really made by the Hand of God. As we compute, it may

just have been the time when, at the Evening-Sacrifice, the officiating Priesthood entered the Holy Place, either to burn the incense or to do other sacred service there. To see before them . . . the Veil of the Holy Place rent from top to bottom . . . and hanging in two parts from its fastenings above and at the side, was, indeed, a terrible portent, which would soon become generally known, and must, in some form or other, have been preserved in tradition. And they all must have understood, that it meant that God's Own Hand had rent the Veil, and for ever deserted and thrown open that Most Holy Place. (*Mortal Messiah*, 4:229–30)

The apostle Paul called attention to another powerful meaning of the tearing of the veil of the Temple on that Friday afternoon two thousand years ago. According to Mosaic ritual established long before the Savior was born, once a year the Aaronic high priest passed through the veil of the Temple into the Holy of Holies on the Day of Atonement (*Yom Kippur*) to perform the Mosaic rituals associated with the Atonement. Only the high priest was allowed to enter, for the Holy of Holies represented God's presence. In Paul's symbolic interpretation of the tearing of the veil, the veil represented the physical body, the flesh, of Jesus Christ. The tearing of the veil from top to bottom (Mark 15:38) represented the physical suffering, the atoning sacrifice, the tearing of the Savior's flesh to open the way for all to enter God's presence, to be justified or approved of God, without the yearly mediation of the Aaronic high priest. Christ was the great and last mediator, the great and last sacrifice (D&C 76:69; Alma 34:10). His spilt blood was the fulfillment of the blood of animal sacrifices that the high priest sprinkled in the Holy of Holies. All of this is explained in chapters 9 and 10 of the book of Hebrews, especially the following verses:

> For when Moses had spoken every precept to all the people according to the law, he took the blood of calves and of goats, with water, and scarlet wool, and hyssop, and sprinkled both the book, and all the people,
>
> Saying, This is the blood of the testament which God hath enjoined unto you.
>
> Moreover he sprinkled with blood both the tabernacle, and all the vessels of the ministry.
>
> And almost all things are by the law purged with blood; and without shedding of blood is no remission.
>
> It was therefore necessary that the patterns of things in the heavens should be purified with these; but the heavenly things themselves with better sacrifices than these.
>
> For Christ is not entered into the holy places made with hands, which are the figures of the true; but into heaven itself, now to appear in the presence of God for us. (Hebrews 9:19–24)
>
> Having therefore, brethren, boldness to enter into the holiest by the blood of Jesus,
>
> By a new and living way, which he hath consecrated for us, through the veil, that is to say, his flesh. (Hebrews 10:19–20)

In our own day, the torn flesh of the Savior is symbolized in the torn bread of the sacrament. By means of this tangible emblem, we remember the Savior's physical, redemptive suffering in Gethsemane and on the cross at Golgotha.

TESTIMONY OF OTHER WITNESSES

Following the testimony of the earth itself, along with the various elements of nature that also cried out and affirmed that this crucified Jesus was indeed the God of the universe, certain members of the party gathered at Golgotha were also deeply affected. Matthew reports that the Roman centurion who supervised the execution and some of those who were with him were impelled to exclaim, "Truly this was the Son of God" (Matthew 27:54). In addition, many women were there, those who had come up with Jesus to Jerusalem from Galilee (Luke 23:49). These were "great and faithful women who followed our Lord and who, for their faith and righteousness, shall be exalted to thrones of glory" (McConkie, *Doctrinal New Testament Commentary*, 1:833). Jesus' other friends ("all his acquaintance"; Luke 23:49) were at Golgotha as well.

No mention is made of any of the apostles being there, except for John. There is no doubt that the original members of the Quorum of the Twelve came to know exactly what happened at Golgotha and also came to know for themselves that Jesus was truly the Son of God. Jesus himself declared to the eleven apostles gathered at the Mount of Ascension after his resurrection that they were witnesses of him (Acts 1:8). Afterward, the apostles bore powerful testimony of their Savior (Acts 4:33). Peter, on the occasion of Cornelius's conversion, declared that the apostles were "witnesses of all things which [Jesus] did both in the land of the Jews, and in Jerusalem; whom they slew and hanged on a tree" (Acts 10:39).

In our own day, the same kind of witness as that possessed by the original apostles regarding the crucifixion has also been affirmed by living apostles and prophets. Elder Harold B. Lee bore his personal witness of the concluding events of the Atonement: "It was a week following the conference, when I was preparing myself for a radio talk on the life of the Savior when I read again the story of the life, the crucifixion and, the resurrection of the Master—there came to me as I read that, a reality of that story, more than just what was on the written page. For in truth, I found myself viewing the scenes with a cer-tainty as though I had been there in person. I know that these things come by the revelations of the living God" (*Divine Revelation*, 12).

Another powerful illustration comes from the 1989 October general conference, when Elder David B. Haight of the Quorum of the Twelve recounted an experience he had had during a recent life-threatening episode. After becoming unconscious, he said, the terrible pain and commotion ceased. He was in a calm and peaceful place. He heard no voices but was conscious of being in a holy presence and atmosphere.

> During the hours and days that followed, there was impressed again and again upon my mind the eternal mission and exalted position of the Son of Man. . . .
>
> I was shown a panoramic view of His earthly ministry. . . .
>
> During those days of unconsciousness I was given, by the gift and power of the Holy Ghost, a more perfect knowledge of His mission. . . . My soul was taught over and over again the events of the betrayal, the mock trial, the scourging of the flesh of even one of the Godhead. I witnessed . . . His being stretched upon [the cross] as it lay on the ground, that the crude spikes could be driven with a mallet into His hands and wrists and

feet to secure His body as it hung on the cross for public display.

Crucifixion—the horrible and painful death which He suffered—was chosen from the beginning. By that excruciating death, He descended below all things, as is recorded, that through His resurrection He would ascend above all things (see D&C 88:6). . . .

I cannot begin to convey to you the deep impact that these scenes have confirmed upon my soul. ("The Sacrament—and the Sacrifice," 59–60)

TYPES, SHADOWS, AND SYMBOLS OF HIS DEATH

Normally the Romans left the bodies of their crucified victims on their crosses to decompose. But Jewish law required the same-day burial of victims so that the land "be not defiled" (Deuteronomy 21:22–23). In the case of Jesus and the two thieves, therefore, Jewish leaders requested of Pilate that the legs of the crucified men be broken to hasten their deaths. They could thus be taken down off the crosses so as not to defile the coming Sabbath, which was also a high holy day (John 19:31). But when the soldiers came to Jesus to break his legs and they saw that he was already dead, "they brake not his legs" and so fulfilled the ancient typology and prophetic symbolism associated with the Paschal lamb (Exodus 12:46). Just as no bone of the Passover lamb was to be broken before it was slaughtered, so no bone of Jesus was broken, as the Psalmist had foreseen (Psalm 34:20). Jesus remained without blemish, as the lamb set aside for the Passover sacrifice was required to be (Exodus 12:5).

Then one of the Roman soldiers who was tending the victims thrust his spear into the side of Jesus, probably to reassure

himself that He really was dead. In so doing, the soldier also fulfilled more ancient prophecy and symbolism. Out of the Savior's
side wound flowed blood and water, indicative of a ruptured
heart. Elder James E. Talmage declares his conviction that the
Lord Jesus died of a "physical rupture of the heart" and provides
ample evidence of this rare but recognized medical condition.
He concludes: "Great mental stress, poignant emotion either of
grief or joy, and intense spiritual struggle are among the recognized causes of heart rupture. The present writer believes that
the Lord Jesus died of a broken heart" (*Jesus the Christ*, 669).
More important, Jesus' death from a broken heart was also foreseen by the Psalmist: "Reproach hath broken my heart; and I
am full of heaviness: and I looked for some to take pity, but
there was none" (Psalm 69:20).

Indeed, Jewish and Roman leaders who contributed to Jesus'
death offered neither help nor pity and thus fulfilled the
prophecy of Psalm 69. But the symbolism of the blood and
water resulting from the Savior's broken heart connects his
atoning death with the specific elements and requirements of
spiritual rebirth: "Inasmuch as ye were born into the world by
water, and blood, and the spirit, which I have made, and so
became of dust a living soul, even so ye must be born again into
the kingdom of heaven, of water, and of the Spirit, and be
cleansed by blood, even the blood of mine Only Begotten"
(Moses 6:59). When Jesus completed the Atonement, he died
of a broken heart, which involved blood and water. If we are to
be born again, we must offer a broken heart, accept the cleansing blood of Jesus Christ, and come up out of the water of bap-
tism (3 Nephi 9:20; Romans 6:3–6).

The blood and the water from the wound in Jesus' side is
also linked to the ancient Jewish tradition of mixing water with

wine for the third cup that was to be drunk during the Passover, or Seder, dinner. This third cup, the "cup after supper" or "cup of blessing," is explicitly associated with the inauguration of the sacrament of the Lord's Supper, which was instituted specifically for participants in the sacrament to remember the blood sacrifice of the Son of God on their behalf (Luke 22:20). Thus, the mixing of water with wine for the third cup of the Passover supper is symbolic of the Messiah's death by a broken heart.

As the Roman soldiers stood at the foot of the cross, no doubt gaping at the wounded side of their victim, a wound made notable by the blood *and* water issuing forth, the prophet Zechariah's ancient prophecy, spoken as though he were the Lord, reached fulfillment: "They shall look upon me whom they have pierced" (Zechariah 12:10). And like other prophetic statements about the Messiah, this declaration will likely see fulfillment again at the Second Coming when the Jewish people will also gape at the same side wound, as well as the wounds in the hands and feet of the Savior, and ask what they mean. And Jesus will reply: "These wounds are the wounds with which I was wounded in the house of my friends. I am he who was lifted up. I am Jesus that was crucified. I am the Son of God" (D&C 45:51–52; Zechariah 13:6).

JOSEPH OF ARIMATHAEA AND JESUS' BURIAL

One of the unsung heroes in the tragic drama of the Savior's death was Joseph of Arimathaea, a member of the Sanhedrin, "an honourable counsellor," and a disciple of the Master who "waited for the kingdom of God" (Mark 15:43; Luke 23:51; Matthew 27:57; John 19:38). Some New Testament students have pointed to a nonscriptural tradition that identifies Joseph of Arimathaea as Jesus' great-uncle, that is, uncle to Jesus' mother, Mary, and brother to Anna, Mary's mother. He is also described as a rich and powerful man, which is in harmony with the scriptures. We cannot prove the family connection described by this tradition, but we are sure that Joseph boldly, even courageously, lobbied Pilate for the Savior's body and then "bought fine linen, and took him down, and wrapped him in the linen" (Mark 15:46). John adds that Nicodemus assisted by purchasing an expensive mixture of myrrh and aloes and helped Joseph prepare the body of Jesus for burial after the manner of the Jews by wrapping his body in the linen cloth with the spices (John 19:39–40).

It took great courage for Joseph to appear before Pilate to procure the Savior's body (Mark 15:43). He was taking a risk to act so boldly before Roman authority, and he was certainly in peril from Jewish leaders and fellow members of the Sanhedrin eager to stamp out the new Jesus movement (Acts 9:2). There was much reason to fear the Jews, as all the disciples knew (John 19:38; 20:19).

That Pilate gave to Joseph the body of Jesus, considering the risks that he in turn was taking in surrendering the corpse of a troublemaker to Jesus' family or close friends, is indicative of at least two things. First, Pilate wanted to avoid further conflict with the Jews by making sure that Jewish concerns over the approaching Sabbath were honored. Second, Pilate really did understand that Jesus was innocent and was willing to allow him a proper, or honorable, burial.

Dishonorable persons, those convicted of the kind of crimes for which Jesus was crucified received tough treatment after death, as Josephus described: "He that blasphemeth God let him be stoned, and let him hang upon a tree all that day, and then let him be buried in an ignominious and obscure manner" (*Antiquities of the Jews*, 4.8.96). On the other hand, an honorable burial is believed to have consisted of washing and anointing the corpse, laying out the body, wrapping it in new cloth and spices, and interring it in a known, high-quality, family tomb (Brown, *Death of the Messiah*, 2:1261). In large measure the body of Jesus was treated this way, and, thus, his innocence and honor were affirmed even in the manner of his burial.

No mention is made in the Gospels of Jesus' body being anointed. Time did not permit the family or the disciples to give Jesus' body the type of anointing appropriate for an honorable man, let alone true royalty. "The preparations had to be hurried, because when the sun had set the Sabbath would have begun. All that they could do, therefore, was to wash the corpse, to lay it amid the spices, to wrap the head in a white napkin, to roll the fine linen round and round the wounded limbs, and to lay the body reverently in the rocky niche" (McConkie, *Mortal Messiah*, 4:239). Five days earlier, however, Mary, sister of Martha, had anointed Jesus at her home, "in token of [his] burial" (JST John 12:7). This action seems most appropriate because the home of the righteous is next to the house of the Lord in sanctity. Additionally, Mark and Luke tell us that certain women did plan to anoint the body of Jesus to insure a proper and honorable burial. "And when the sabbath was past, Mary Magdalene, and Mary the mother of James, and Salome, had bought sweet spices, that they might come and anoint him" (Mark 16:1; Luke 23:55–24:1).

Joseph offered his new, rock-cut tomb located in a garden and laid the lifeless corpse of the Son of God in the never-before-used burial chamber (John 19:41–42). We have the sense that this was also symbolic of royalty. One scholar has pointed out the parallel between Luke's description of the tomb, "wherein never man before was laid" (Luke 23:53), and the phrase he used earlier in his text to describe Jesus' triumphal entry into Jerusalem on a colt, "whereon yet never man sat" (Luke 19:30). "Luke may have favored this particular expression, 'where no one was yet laid,' as an echo of the clause he had used to describe the entry of Jesus as king into Jerusalem on a colt 'on which no person has ever sat' (19:30, 28). . . . there was a regal character to the burial in [the Gospel of] John" (Brown, *Death of the Messiah*, 2:1255).

Just as the new colt was symbolic of royalty, so too was the new tomb symbolic of royalty. Jesus was the Great King. He was also literally King of the Jews. The fulness of the earth was his; the interment of a Jewish monarch was his due. And yet he had been treated and executed as if he were a criminal. Again, we note the irony here as well. Jesus was condemned to die by the vehemence of the Jewish council, and yet he was laid to rest in the tomb of one of the most honorable members of that council (Mark 15:43). Matthew and Mark report that as a final act Joseph rolled a great stone to the door of the sepulchre and departed (Matthew 27:60; Mark 15:46).

All of this was pure, unadulterated, selfless service. Preparing another person's lifeless body for burial is a true act of kindness and charity, because it is one thing that can never be repaid by the individual being served. It can be done without expectation of recompense. Such was the largeness of soul possessed by Joseph of Arimathaea.

Another "ruler of the Jews" (John 3:1) also volunteered his time and substantial means to help bury the lifeless body of the Messiah. He was Nicodemus, the same man who was a member of the Sanhedrin, who had earlier gone to Jesus by night (John

3:2), who revered him as a rabbinic master (John 3:2), and who had defended the Savior against the illegal machinations of the chief priests and Pharisees (John 7:45–52). It is not hard to envision the initially reticent Nicodemus experiencing the transforming power of Christ to the extent that he felt moved upon to participate in the burial of his Lord. The Gospel of John alone tells us that Nicodemus not only accompanied his colleague Joseph of Arimathaea but also purchased a sizable quantity of myrrh and aloes to prepare Jesus' body for burial (John 19:39). This was a very large, costly amount, representative of what was used in royal burials, and is another indication that Jesus' kingly status was acknowledged symbolically (2 Chronicles 16:14).

Both Joseph of Arimathea and Nicodemus were righteous leaders of the Jews who recognized the special nature of the Savior's life and teachings. They remained loyal to him and performed a special act of love and respect. The actions they took in association with the Savior's burial, once again, fulfilled prophecy. Isaiah had said the Messiah would be "with the rich in his death" (Isaiah 53:9), and so he was.

The final act in the drama of Golgotha culminated in the placement of guards at the Garden Tomb. This was done to satisfy the concerns of the chief priests and Pharisees that the disciples of Jesus be prevented from stealing his body and making it look like Jesus had come alive again, as he had prophesied. Several ironies emerge in this scene. First, the Jewish leaders had no qualms about going to the Gentile leader, Pilate, on the day after the crucifixion, a special and most sacred Sabbath day (John 19:31). They wanted to ensure the ultimate success of their conspiracy, even though it brought upon them ritual defilement, and they had gone to great lengths to remain ritually pure in other matters of Jewish life. "By personally arranging for the watch and sealing the tomb, the chief priests and Pharisees, according to their own tradition, suffered defilement" (McConkie, *Doctrinal New Testament Commentary*, 1:838). Second, in speaking to Pilate, they referred to Jesus as "that deceiver," when they themselves were guilty of the ultimate deceptions (Matthew 27:63). And third, the Jewish leaders—the inveterate enemies of Christ, as Elder Talmage calls them—had paid close attention to the words of the Savior about his resurrection, but those words had no spiritual effect on them, even though they were charged to be the spiritual guardians of their people (*Jesus the Christ*, 665–66).

Following Pilate's terse retort to Jewish leaders that they could make the tomb of Jesus as secure as they pleased, the leaders of the Jews placed an armed guard at the sepulchre and affixed some kind of a seal between the great stone and the portal of the tomb. Undoubtedly, both the Roman and Jewish leaders hoped that this would be the end of their problems.

To the apostles, disciples, and friends of Jesus who had been watching and waiting for the end to come, who were still at Golgotha when the Savior expired, and who were wrung out physically, emotionally, and spiritually by the events of that terrible Friday, the next day must have been the darkest of days. Their own sorrow and anguish must have been beyond words; their grief and uncertainty over the future, overwhelming. The crucifixion and suffering of one so compassionate and pure as Jesus of Nazareth was a horrible sight. It was compounded by Jesus' claim to be the Messiah, the Son of God, and the Redeemer of the children of men. And yet he seemed to die the ignominious death of a common criminal and an enemy of

Rome. The apostles, disciples, family members, and friends of Jesus had invested their whole lives in him. Now he was gone.

But Friday and Saturday were not the end of the story for the disciples then nor for disciples now. From the long hours of gloom, depression, and despondency came a morning of brilliant hope and complete triumph for the Savior's associates, a joy and gladness more glorious than was their deepest despair. How grateful we ought to be that there is a grand sequel in the story of God's infinite love for humankind and mercy toward each one. Truly, the story and the effects of the Atonement never end.

Behold I have given unto you my gospel, and this is the gospel which I have given unto you—that I came into the world to do the will of my Father, because my Father sent me.

And my Father sent me that I might be lifted up upon the cross; and after that I had been lifted up upon the cross, that I might draw all men unto me, that as I have been lifted up by men even so should men be lifted up by the Father, to stand before me, to be judged of their works, whether they be good or whether they be evil.

3 Nephi 27:13–14

CHAPTER 12

The Doctrine of the Cross

What was begun in the Garden of Gethsemane was consummated on the cross of Golgotha. Two times the Savior shed his blood for you and for me. In two places he endured this ghastly physical suffering to pay for our sins as well as our sorrows, sufferings, sicknesses, and fallen condition, even our mortality. The Savior himself acknowledged both Gethsemane and Golgotha, the bleeding from every pore (D&C 19:18; Luke 22:44) and the crucifixion (D&C 35:2; 138:35). Both the garden and the cross are integral parts of his atoning sacrifice.

The Cross

For Latter-day Saints the symbol of the cross of Christ is as important, is as much a part of our theology, as it is for other Christians. Though latter-day prophets, under divine inspiration, have chosen not to display or portray material representations of the cross (icons) in our buildings of worship, the symbol of the cross of Christ still bids us to do as Christ did:

1. To forgive all men (D&C 64:10)

2. To extend mercy to others—that we may obtain mercy (3 Nephi 12:7; D&C 88:40)

3. To put others before ourselves and serve one another (Mosiah 2:17)

4. To take up our crosses and follow him (Matthew 10:38; Luke 9:23)

5. To endure all things with patience and dignity (D&C 67:13; 1 Peter 2:23)

The image of the cross of Christ lies at the heart of the foundational document of our religion—the Book of Mormon. In describing his early visions, the prophet Nephi testified that he "saw that [the Lamb of God] was lifted up upon the cross and slain for the sins of the world" (1 Nephi 11:33). But the capstone testimony regarding the cross came approximately six hundred years later when another Nephi reported the New World visitation of the very God of whom Lehi's son Nephi had prophesied. The resurrected Lord Jesus Christ affirmed to his American Israelites that he had come into the world to do his Father's will: "My Father sent me that I might be lifted up upon the cross; and after that I had been lifted up upon the cross, that I might draw all men unto me, that as I have been lifted up by men even so should men be lifted up by the Father, to stand before me, to be judged of their works, whether they be good or whether they be evil" (3 Nephi 27:14).

The cross was an important image and symbol to many prophets in different dispensations across time. The earliest mention of the cross was made by the prophet Enoch, sixth from Adam, who saw in vision "the Son of Man lifted up on the cross, after the manner of men" (Moses 7:55). Enoch also saw all the creations of God mourn at the crucifixion (Moses 7:56).

It is difficult to imagine that Adam, the first man, did not also have some knowledge of the crucifixion. He was taught about altar offerings and their similitude of the sacrifice of the Only Begotten (Moses 5:5–7). And he prophesied what would happen to his posterity unto the latest generation (D&C 107:56).

To the brother of Jared great things were revealed, including a knowledge of the cross, as Moroni recorded: "And the Lord commanded the brother of Jared to go down out of the mount from the presence of the Lord, and write the things which he had seen; and they were forbidden to come unto the children of men until after that he should be lifted up upon the cross; and for this cause did king Mosiah keep them, that they should not come unto the world until after Christ should show himself unto his people" (Ether 4:1).

In the meridian dispensation, just a few years after the Savior's death, the cross of Jesus Christ became for Christian disciples one of the most profound symbols of his suffering and atoning sacrifice. That was particularly true for the apostle Paul, who would not "glory [boast], save in the cross of our Lord Jesus Christ" (Galatians 6:14), for it was by the cross that God and man were reconciled (Ephesians 2:16). In a powerful image presented to the Corinthian Saints, Paul declared that "the preaching of the cross" was the very "power of God" unto those of us who are saved (1 Corinthians 1:18).

In the dispensation of the fulness of times, President Joseph F. Smith received a panoramic vision of the spirit world and the Savior's ministry to it. The Savior did not go in person to preach the everlasting gospel unto the wicked and rebellious (D&C 138:20–21). Messengers from among the righteous in the spirit world went instead (D&C 138:30–31). "It was made known among the dead, both small and great, the unrighteous as well as the faithful, that redemption had been wrought through the sacrifice of the Son of God upon the cross" (D&C 138:35). Thus we see that the cross was preached beyond the veil.

TAKING UP OUR CROSSES

One of the most powerful uses of the image of the cross in Restoration scripture concerns the invitation, even command, to take up one's cross and follow the Savior. To the Nephite multitude assembled at the temple in the land Bountiful, the Savior described some of the wicked ideas and attitudes his people should never allow to enter their hearts, and then he said: "For it is better that ye should deny yourselves of these things, wherein ye will take up your cross, than that ye should be cast into hell" (3 Nephi 12:30).

In his mortal ministry, the Savior had explained to his disciples in the Old World that for one to take up his cross meant "to deny himself all ungodliness, and every worldly lust, and keep my commandments" (JST Matthew 16:26). The Savior added another significant qualifier and definition to the phrase "take up your cross" when he spoke to Joseph Knight in April 1830: "Behold, I manifest unto you, Joseph Knight, by these words, that you must take up your cross, in the which you must pray vocally before the world as well as in secret, and in your family, and among your friends, and in all places" (D&C 23:6).

To take up one's cross is to adopt the Savior's pattern of living, to think as he thinks, to eschew unworthy thoughts, to pray as he prays, to testify as he testifies, to proclaim truth boldly to the world as he proclaims truth boldly without concern for what the world will think of him. And if we do these things, the consequences of our actions will turn out to be beyond our fondest hopes and dreams—the joy and glory of eternal life. The Book of Mormon prophet Jacob emphasized the need for us to pay no heed to what the world may say or think of us as we press forward in Christ, living lives of quiet dignity in the face of sufferings, tribulations, and persecutions—even being chided for our very convictions and way of life because, after all, "we aren't really Christian," according to some. Said Jacob: "But, behold, the righteous, the saints of the Holy One of Israel, they who have believed in the Holy One of Israel, they who have endured the crosses of the world, and despised the shame of it, they shall inherit the kingdom of God, which was prepared for them from the foundation of the world, and their joy shall be full forever" (2 Nephi 9:18).

Jacob's language immediately recalls the image of the Savior on the cross, enduring unimaginable pain, suffering, and hardship, being the object of ridicule and shame, and yet accepting all of it with quiet dignity. The phrase used by Jacob, "despised the shame of it," is intriguing. I take him to be saying that one of the profound ways we endure our own crosses is by regarding the ridicule or views of the world as "negligible, worthless, or distasteful," which is one of the definitions of the word *despise*. We will treat the shame or ridicule of the world as being of no account. In fact, if we are truly imitating the Savior on the cross, we will not just accept what is dished out but will do as he did: "Not rendering evil for evil, or railing for railing: but contrariwise blessing; knowing that ye are thereunto called, that ye should inherit a blessing" (1 Peter 3:9).

The apostle Paul is a powerful example of one who took up his cross and despised the shame of it, rendering blessing for railing. He testified:

We are fools for Christ's sake, but ye are wise in Christ; we are weak, but ye are strong; ye are honourable, but we are despised.

Even unto this present hour we both hunger, and thirst, and are naked, and are buffeted, and have no certain dwelling place;

And labour, working with our own hands: being reviled, we bless; being persecuted, we suffer it:

Being defamed, we intreat: we are made as the filth of the world, and are the offscouring of all things unto this day. (1 Corinthians 4:10–13)

Shame and ridicule come in subtle forms these days. They can become a part of our own attitudes without our even realizing it. Sometimes they take the form of pity for others because of their weaknesses, handicaps, or misfortunes, real or perceived. Sometimes they come in the form of looking down on individuals because their economic circumstances have taken a turn for the worse. Sometimes they come in the form of intrusive attempts to "help" bring people up to "our level" socially and culturally or educate them or disabuse them of their naive ways. I am persuaded that just as we hope that the ridicule of the world towards us will be tempered, so we must examine our attitudes to make sure that pride, egocentrism, and self-importance do not put us into the category of those who ridicule—even subtly. We never know when life will turn the tables on us, when our lives will take a downturn, and we will be facing other burdens of the cross.

REVERENCE FOR THE CROSS

The cross of Christ is a powerful symbol and image for us as Latter-day Saints. Through the image of the cross, the Savior himself bids us to follow him in every way and in every thing. The image of the cross ought to evoke in us the deepest feelings of gratitude for what the Savior did—and did for all of us—individually as well as collectively.

Several years ago, President Gordon B. Hinckley told a story that helps us understand and appreciate just what the Savior did for all of us. That story was retold by President James E. Faust in a magnificent address entitled "The Atonement: Our Greatest Hope." The setting for the story was a one-room schoolhouse in the mountains of Virginia where the boys were so rough no teacher had been able to handle them.

> Then one day an inexperienced young teacher applied. He was told that every teacher had received an awful beating, but the teacher accepted the risk. The first day of school the teacher asked the boys to establish their own rules and the penalty for breaking the rules. The class came up with 10 rules, which were written on the blackboard. Then the teacher asked, "What shall we do with one who breaks the rules?"
>
> "Beat him across the back ten times without his coat on," came the response.
>
> A day or so later, . . . the lunch of a big student, named Tom, was stolen. The thief was located—a little hungry fellow, about ten years old.
>
> As Little Jim came up to take his licking, he pleaded to keep his coat on. "Take your coat off," the teacher said. "You helped make the rules!"
>
> The boy took off the coat. He had no shirt and revealed a bony little crippled body. As the teacher

hesitated with the rod, Big Tom jumped to his feet and volunteered to take the boy's licking.

"Very well, there is a certain law that one can become a substitute for another. Are you all agreed?" the teacher asked.

After five strokes across Tom's back, the rod broke. The class was sobbing. Little Jim had reached up and caught Tom with both arms around his neck. "Tom, I'm sorry that I stole your lunch, but I was awful hungry. Tom, I will love you till I die for taking my licking for me! Yes, I will love you forever!"

President Faust then said that after telling the story, President Hinckley quoted Isaiah: "Surely he hath borne our griefs, and carried our sorrows. . . . He was wounded for our transgressions, he was bruised for our iniquities: the chastisement of our peace was upon him; and with his stripes we are healed" (Isaiah 53:4–5).

Continuing, President Faust declared:

No man knows the full weight of what our Savior bore, but by the power of the Holy Ghost we can know something of the supernal gift He gave us. In the words of our sacrament hymn:

> *We may not know, we cannot tell,*
> *What pains he had to bear,*
> *But we believe it was for us*
> *He hung and suffered there.*
> [Hymns, no. 194, "There Is a Green Hill
> Far Away"] (Ensign, November 2001, 18–19)

Our freedom, our relief, our redemption from the crushing

pain we deserve on account of our sins came at a dear price, not to us but to the One Perfect Being who ever walked the earth. Because of him, we don't get what we deserve! He alone took our punishment. Like Big Tom in our story, he took what would have come to us without his intervention.

Jesus said that he trod the winepress alone. None were with him when he "took our licking," not even his own Father, who withdrew his Spirit from his Son while the Son was on the cross. There, on the cross, the Savior of his own free will took to himself our stains and our sins, as well as the blood and sins of all generations (Jacob 1:19; 2 Nephi 9:44). Alma reminds us that without the Atonement operating in our lives, we would have to "stand before the bar of God, having [our] garments stained with blood and all manner of filthiness" (Alma 5:22). In the garden and on the cross Jesus initiated the great exchange: He cleansed our garments and imputed our stains and blood to his garments. That is why when he comes again, at the great and terrible second coming, he will be wearing red garments:

> And it shall be said: Who is this that cometh down from God in heaven with dyed garments; yea, from the regions which are not known, clothed in his glorious apparel, traveling in the greatness of his strength?
>
> And he shall say: I am he who spake in righteousness, mighty to save.
>
> And the Lord shall be red in his apparel, and his garments like him that treadeth in the wine-vat. (D&C 133:46–48)

Red is the color of stains that accrue to a person's garments when working in a winepress. Red is also symbolic of the

Savior's spilled blood in Gethsemane and on the cross. Red becomes symbolic of victory—victory over the devil, hell, and endless torment. At the Second Coming, Jesus Christ will be recognized as the ultimate victor by his wearing red garments. Also at the Second Coming, all shall recognize the Savior by the wounds he has chosen to retain in his hands and feet, which wounds he received on the cross. Even those who have been unable to know the Lord because of what certain leaders of their people did long ago will receive the blessing of knowing their Redeemer:

> And then shall the Jews look upon me and say: What are these wounds in thine hands and in thy feet?
>
> Then shall they know that I am the Lord; for I will say unto them: These wounds are the wounds with which I was wounded in the house of my friends. I am he who was lifted up. I am Jesus that was crucified. I am the Son of God.
>
> And then shall they weep because of their iniquities; then shall they lament because they persecuted their king.
>
> And then shall the heathen nations be redeemed, and they that knew no law shall have part in the first resurrection; and it shall be tolerable for them. (D&C 45:51–54)

Truly, the cross is a powerful and lasting symbol of the Savior's all-encompassing atonement.

Last but not least, the marks of the cross are at the center of the most profound expressions of our worship of the Savior. These expressions are reserved for our most sacred places of worship. We renew our commitment to remember the cross of

Christ, and, in a sense, we renew our commitment to take up our crosses when we worship in the house of the Lord. Temples are one more evidence of how serious Latter-day Saints are about remembering the cross. Almost twenty-eight centuries ago, Jehovah promised Israel that he would never forget his people: "Behold, I have graven thee upon the palms of my hands" (Isaiah 49:16; 1 Nephi 21:16). In turn, this prophetic reference to the marks of the crucifixion bids us, the Lord's people—latter-day Israel—never to forget him.

THE LIVING CHRIST

Some have asked, "If the cross is such an important image and symbol, why don't the Latter-day Saints honor it more, wear it, or display it in their homes and churches?" There may be several parts to the answer.

First, there is the danger that any symbol of the Savior, whom we worship, may itself become the thing venerated when it is made into a tangible artifact, as ancient Israel demonstrated. Moses set up the brass serpent in the wilderness as a type and symbol of the Messiah (1 Nephi 17:41; 2 Nephi 25:20; Alma 33:18–22; Helaman 8:13–15; John 3:14–15). But after many hundreds of years, the symbol had become the thing being worshiped and had to be destroyed by righteous King Hezekiah (2 Kings 18:4).

Second, even though the cross was a powerful theological symbol and image to the earliest Christians, the idea of wearing a replica of the tool of crucifixion probably would have seemed abhorrent.

Third, modern prophets have encouraged us to keep images of the living Christ uppermost in our minds and live lives worthy of his presence. In this connection Elder Gordon B. Hinckley related the following story many years ago:

> We recently held an open house in the Arizona Temple. Following a complete renovation of that building, nearly a quarter of a million people saw its beautiful interior. On the first day of the opening, clergymen of other religions were invited as special guests, and hundreds responded. It was my privilege to speak to them and to answer their questions at the conclusion of their tours. I told them that we would be pleased to answer any queries they might have. Many were asked. Among these was one which came from a Protestant minister.
>
> Said he: "I've been all through this building, this temple which carries on its face the name of Jesus Christ, but nowhere have I seen any representation of the cross, the symbol of Christianity. I have noted your buildings elsewhere and likewise find an absence of the cross. Why is this when you say you believe in Jesus Christ?"
>
> I responded: "I do not wish to give offense to any of my Christian brethren who use the cross on the steeples of their cathedrals and at the altars of their chapels, who wear it on their vestments and imprint in on their books and other literature. But for us, the cross is the symbol of the dying Christ, while our message is a declaration of the living Christ."
>
> He then asked: "If you do not use the cross, what is the symbol of your religion?"
>
> I replied that the lives of our people must become

the only meaningful expression of our faith and, in fact, therefore, the symbol of our worship. ("Symbol of Christ," 92)

President Harold B. Lee taught the same principle through an experience he related:

> At the World's Fair in New York, President G. Stanley McAllister, of the New York Stake, told us of an experience that he had that probably defines the distinction that I am trying to make. He was on a plane returning from a business assignment in St. Louis and his seatmate was a Catholic priest. As they flew toward New York and became acquainted with each other, each discovered the other's identity as to church relationships. As they talked about various things, the Catholic priest said, "Have you been to the World's Fair?" "Yes," Brother McAllister said, "I am on the committee that helped to plan our pavilion." "Well, have you visited our Catholic exhibit?" And again Brother McAllister said yes. The priest said, "Well, I have been to the fair and I have visited your exhibit. At the Catholic exhibit we have the dead Christ—the *Pieta*. But the Mormon Pavilion has the live Christ, or the living Christ." And in that I think there is a distinguishing difference. (*Stand Ye in Holy Places*, 149–50)

Living prophets have asked that we emphasize, think of, and live our lives bathed in the light of the living Christ. The living Christ signals that the heavens are not sealed. They are open, and revelation continues daily. That revelation continues to reveal the mind of Christ to each one of us.

SOME FINAL THOUGHTS

Long after money, power, and prestige—the fleeting trinkets and treasures of the world—have slipped away and mean nothing, the actions of our Lord in Gethsemane and on the cross will grow in stature and mean everything to us. The image of Jesus, bloody, bruised and humiliated, stumbling along while attempting to bear the weight of the cross, finally reaching Golgotha and being nailed to the cruel cross of crucifixion, in many ways symbolizes and encapsulates the profound lessons we need to learn in this mortal existence. Under the most adverse circumstances, the Savior moved along the course that would take him to the completion of his mission. What happened to him did not come because Pilate or the Jewish leaders had the power to impose it but because he was willing to accept it (Packer, Conference Report, April 1988, 80). Through it all he was loyal to the Father.

Faithfully bearing up under our loads and facing our trials and tribulations while at the same time resolving to serve God at all hazards and accept his will moulds us and makes us fit for the kingdom of God. When we submit to that which God sees fit to inflict, we become like the Savior. In fact, we cannot enjoy the association of the Savior without offering sacrifice in the similitude of the Savior, suffering tribulation in his name (D&C 138:12–13). The *Lectures on Faith* tell us that "the faith necessary unto life and salvation never could be obtained without the sacrifice of all earthly things," for "it is in vain for persons to fancy to themselves that they are heirs with those, or can be heirs with them, who have offered their all in sacrifice, and by this means obtained faith in God and favor with him so as to obtain eternal life, unless they, in like manner, offer unto him the same sacrifice, and through that offering obtain the knowledge that they are accepted of him" (6:7–8).

When we have determined that we are willing to sacrifice all we possess, we are actually living lives in the similitude of Jesus of Nazareth: We are living lives of consecration. Taking up our crosses and living lives of consecration are really synonymous. We need only look around us (and not very long at that) to find individuals whose lives are reflections of the Savior's premier sacrifice. They make us want to do our very best out of appreciation for their personal examples as well as the Lord's.

A couple my wife and I know put the Lord first and accepted a call to preside over a Latter-day Saint mission in a faraway country. Within the first weeks of their service, they encountered serious challenges that had to be dealt with. And within the first year, the husband's father died, the wife's father died, and their first child was married—all back in the United States. Of course, the husband, who was the mission president, could not leave the mission. He did not flounder or complain. He did what the Lord asked because he had consecrated his life to the Master. When I think of him, I think of the Savior, and I want to be better and to do better. In this man I see glimpses of the kind of "character and capacity and the purity to endure what the Atonement required of Him," to use Elder Neal A. Maxwell's phrase (quoted in Weaver, "God Will Protect Us," 3).

How profoundly grateful I am for a Savior who shows us the way in so many ways. In the Sermon on the Mount, he tells us that we are to be the salt and the light of the world (Matthew 5:13–14). As Robert Sloan, president of Baylor University, points out, "Salt and light extend their influences

197

to their environment" ("Character of Leadership," 29). Like-wise, character influences its environment. As the Savior is the Salt and the Light of the World, so we as his disciples are called upon to possess the character he possesses and then to influence the world—as do salt and light. In other words, we are to take up our crosses and follow him. After all is said and done, we must follow the Savior at all hazards, for he is not just our best hope, he is our only hope.

Sources

The Anchor Bible Dictionary. Edited by David Noel Freedman. 6 vols. New York: Doubleday, 1992.

Andrus, Hyrum L. *God, Man, and the Universe*. Vol. 1 of *Foundations of the Millennial Kingdom of Christ*. Salt Lake City: Deseret Book, 1968.

Avigad, Nahman. *Discovering Jerusalem*. Nashville: Thomas Nelson, 1983.

Brown, Raymond E. *The Death of the Messiah*. Garden City, N.Y.: Doubleday, 1994.

Bruce, F. F. *New Testament History*. Garden City, N.Y.: Doubleday, 1980.

Davis, C. Truman. "A Physician Testifies about Crucifixion." *The Review of the News*, April 14, 1976.

Clark, J. Reuben, Jr. *As Ye Sow*. Brigham Young University Speeches of the Year, Provo, Utah, May 3, 1955, in J. Reuben Clark Jr., *Behold the Lamb of God* (Salt Lake City: Deseret Book), 1991.

Edwards, William, et al. "On the Physical Death of Jesus Christ." *JAMA [Journal of the American Medical Association]*, March 21, 1986.

Farrar, Frederic W. *The Life of Christ*. New York: Cassell and Company, 1902.

Faust, James E. "The Atonement: Our Greatest Hope." *Ensign*, November 2001.

Galbraith, David B., D. Kelly Ogden, and Andrew C. Skinner. *Jerusalem, the Eternal City*. Salt Lake City: Deseret Book, 1996.

Haight, David B. "The Sacrament—and the Sacrifice." *Ensign*, November 1989.

Hales, Robert D. "Behold, We Count Them Happy Which Endure." *Ensign*, May 1998.

———. "Faith through Tribulation Brings Peace and Joy." *Ensign*, May 2003.

Hall, John F. *New Testament Witnesses of Christ*. American Fork, Utah: Covenant Communications, 2002.

Harper's Bible Dictionary. Edited by Paul J. Achtemeier et al. San Francisco: Harper and Row, 1985.

Hinckley, Bryant S. *Sermons and Missionary Services of Melvin Joseph Ballard*. Salt Lake City: Deseret Book, 1949.

Hinckley, Gordon B. "The Symbol of Christ." *Ensign*, May 1975.

———. *Teachings of Gordon B. Hinckley*. Salt Lake City: Deseret Book, 1997.

Hunter, Howard W. "Eternal Investments." Address to Church Educational System personnel, Salt Lake City, February 10, 1989.

Interpreter's Dictionary of the Bible: An Illustrated Encyclopedia. Nashville: Abingdon Press, 1962.

Journal of Discourses. 26 vols. London: Latter-day Saints' Book Depot, 1854–86.

Josephus, Flavius. *The Antiquities of the Jews* and *The Wars of the Jews*. In *Josephus: Complete Works*. Translated by William Whiston. Grand Rapids, Mich.: Kregel Publications, 1960.

Kimball, Spencer W. *Faith Precedes the Miracle*. Salt Lake City: Deseret Book, 1972.

———. *The Miracle of Forgiveness*. Salt Lake City: Bookcraft, 1969.

———. *Peter, My Brother*. Brigham Young University Speeches of the Year, Provo, 13 July 1971, cited in *The Life and Teachings of Jesus and His Apostles*, 2d ed. (Salt Lake City: The Church of Jesus Christ of Latter-day Saints, 1978).

Klein, Mina C., and H. Arthur Klein. *Temple beyond Time: The Story of the Site of Solomon's Temple at Jerusalem*. New York: Van Nostrand Reinhold, 1970.

Kofford, Cree-L. "The Trial of Christ." In *Clark Memorandum*. Provo, Utah: Brigham Young University, J. Reuben Clark Law School, Fall 2003.

Lee, Harold B. Conference Report, October 1973.

———. *Divine Revelation*. Brigham Young University Speeches of the Year, Provo, Utah, 1952, cited in *The Life and Teachings of Jesus and His Apostles*, 2d ed. (Salt Lake City: The Church of Jesus Christ of Latter-day Saints, 1978).

———. *Stand Ye in Holy Places*. Salt Lake City: Deseret Book, 1974.

Lewis, C. S. *A Grief Observed*. San Francisco: HarperCollins, 1961.

———. *Mere Christianity*. New York: Simon & Schuster, 1996.

Life and Teachings of Jesus and His Apostles. 2d ed. Salt Lake City: The Church of Jesus Christ of Latter-day Saints, 1979.

MacArthur, John F., Jr. *The Murder of Jesus*. Nashville: Word Publishing, 2000.

Maxwell, Neal A. *All These Things Shall Give Thee Experience*. Salt Lake City: Deseret Book, 1979.

———. *Lord, Increase Our Faith*. Salt Lake City: Bookcraft, 1994.

———. "Why Not Now?" *Ensign*, November 1974.

———. "Yet Thou Art There." *Ensign*, November 1987.

McConkie, Bruce R. *Doctrinal New Testament Commentary*. 3 vols. Salt Lake City: Bookcraft, 1965–73.

———. *Mormon Doctrine*. 2d ed. Salt Lake City: Bookcraft, 1966.

———. *The Mortal Messiah*. 4 vols. Salt Lake City: Deseret Book, 1981.

———. "The Purifying Power of Gethsemane." *Ensign*, May 1985.

Mouw, Richard J. "Christian Responses to a World in Crisis." *Fuller Focus*, Spring 2002.

Packer, Boyd K. Conference Report, April 1988.

Peterson, H. Donl, and Charles D. Tate Jr., eds. *The Pearl of Great Price: Revelations from God*. Provo, Utah: Brigham Young University, Religious Studies Center, 1989.

Philo. *Legatio ad Gaium*. See, for example, *Philonis Alexandrini: Legatio ad Gaium*, translated by E. Mary Smallwood (Leiden: E. J. Brill, 1970).

Plautus, Titus Maccius. *The Braggart Warrior*. Translated by Paul Nixon. New York: G. P. Putnam's Sons, 1916.

Powers, Tom. "Treasures in the Storeroom." *Biblical Archaeology Review*, July-August 2003.

Pratt, Parley P., Jr. *Autobiography of Parley P. Pratt*. Revised edition. Edited by Scot Facer Proctor and Maurine Jensen Proctor. Salt Lake City: Deseret Book, 2000.

Sloan, Robert, Jr. "The Character of Leadership." *BYU Magazine*, Winter 2003.

Smith, Joseph. *Lectures on Faith*. Salt Lake City: Deseret Book, 1985.

———. *Teachings of the Prophet Joseph Smith*. Selected by Joseph Fielding Smith. Salt Lake City: Deseret Book, 1976.

Smith, Joseph F. *Gospel Doctrine*. Salt Lake City: Deseret Book, 1968.

Smith, Joseph Fielding. *Doctrines of Salvation*. Compiled by Bruce R. McConkie. 3 vols. Salt Lake City: Bookcraft, 1954–56.

St. Peter "in Gallicantu" "at the Cockcrow" [leaflet]. Jerusalem: Augustinian Fathers of the Assumption (Assumptionists), n.d.

Talmage, James E. *Jesus the Christ*. Salt Lake City: Deseret Book, 1962.

Taylor, John. *John Taylor*, vol. 4 of *Teachings of Presidents of the Church* series. Salt Lake City: The Church of Jesus Christ of Latter-day Saints, 2001.

Tractate Sanhedrin, Chapters 9–11. Vol. 23c of *The Talmud of Babylonia: An American Translation*. Translated by Jacob Neusner. Chico, Calif.: Scholars Press, 1985.

Weaver, Sarah Jane. "God Will Protect Us in These Perilous Times." *Church News*, February 22, 2003.

Wilkinson, John. *Jerusalem As Jesus Knew It*. London: Thames and Hudson, 1978.

Zias, Joseph, and Eliezer Sekeles. "The Crucified Man from Giv'at ha-Mitvar—A Reappraisal." *Biblical Archaeologist*, September 1985.

Index